Thanks to my dad.

THE MUSCLE

Neil Cummins

NEW HOLLAND

Contents

Foreword

My acquaintance with Neil and Mariana was by chance. I first met them at a bridal exhibition in January 2010. My tiny stall was bustling with couples seeking information about my services as a Master of Ceremonies and entertainer for wedding receptions. While attending to others, I could see this giant man with an absolutely stunning partner approaching. They stopped to enquire about my services, casually leaving their details and slowly making their way through the exhibition without any fuss to see the fashion parade. For some reason I wanted this gig.

Shortly after the exhibition I heard from Mariana and I was really pleased to lock in the date for me to host and perform at their wedding reception on Sunday 21 November 2010. At this stage I still had no idea who they were. It was only when I was working with the wedding coordinator that I was told who they were and who some of the guests would be. I was given a rough wedding plan, which included a lot of security, and I was thinking to myself 'How will I survive the night with these guys? Six security guards patrolling the premises and everything needs to be covered so everyone can see the events of the reception'.

In August 2010, I met Neil and Mariana to go over all the requirements needed for the wedding reception. We had a chat about the structure of the evening and the events which would take place. I needed to ask what exactly they did for a living. From memory, Mariana told me she was in property management as a real estate agent and Neil—he quietly informed me that worked for John Ibrahim as one of his personal security staff. That made sense as to why this wedding was so detailed and private; a closed wedding ceremony and a closed wedding reception. I was briefed on the intricate plans for this day and how the wedding was going to be covered by *OK!* magazine the following week with exclusive rights to the story, which was why this was a strictly confidential event. With all these guidelines there was always one thing which Neil would consistently say at this meeting. He kep repeating there were to be no interruptions by anybody and the wedding should be about keeping Mariana and the guests safe. In a calm and respectful manner, he would repeat this several times over the course of the night. It's public knowledge that things for Neil have been up and down and he has chosen a profession where only the strong survive. So here I was sitting opposite a beast of a man best known on the streets as 'The Muscle' and yet all he can think of is protecting his wife-to-be and those attending their very special day. Quite romantic I'd say!

It's not my position as an MC or entertainer to question a client about why they want certain things; I simply respect their wishes and try to make it happen. I look after those who hire me—everyone has their vulnerabilities. At the time of my meeting with Neil and Mariana, I had just finished shooting the third series of *Underbelly: The Golden Mile* where I played Sam Ibrahim under the alias of Harry 'Hammer' Hamoud, guardian angel and eldest brother to nightclub owner John Ibrahim. When I played this character I was always trying to find a vulnerable side to this notorious man yet still make him a believable character. Something that the character I played and Neil share is that they both 'served to protect' those around them no matter the consequences. This is something that Neil knows only too well having lived and breathed this way of life from a young age. This gentle giant, to those within his circle, will always be under his wing. The wedding ... you'll just need to see the photos and they'll tell the story.

Salvatore Coco
    Actor

Foreword

The first time I stepped into DCM's was in 2005. My mates and I decided to kick on and try out a new club, so we rocked up to Oxford Street ub the early hours of the morning. A couple of bouncers were on the door as we approached, they had spotted us crossing the road and eyed us out. I had a feeling that I was going to struggle to get in because of my haircut, piercings and tattoos.

As we reached the entrance of DCM's, this giant of a bouncer nodded his head and said, 'Sorry boys, no chance.' I could hear the beat of the music pumping and was dying to walk into this club. I was so disappointed to get knocked back, it was written all over my face and the bouncer realised this, but he didn't change his mind about letting me in.

I was nice about the whole situation, I didn't want to mess with this guy—he was triple my size—and he looked scary. I asked him what his name was. He asked me why I wanted to know? I introduced myself as Rob and said I was just trying to have a conversation. But he said, 'I don't want to talk to mate.' I asked again if I could go in, but he was like, 'Mate I said no chance the first time, why would I change my mind? Get a haircut and come back and see me.' I laugh about it now.

I ended up leaving that night, but decided to keep trying week after week. I finally saw the nice side of Neil. He thought I had done my time, sitting at the café next door to DCM's. Neil walked over to me and all he said was 'You want to come in? Get a hat to cover your hair.' The DCM's ride had started!

Foreword

DCM'S is definitely the best club I've ever been to, and I'm a party animal! Nothing beats DCM's—whoever has experienced it will understand what I mean, especially when the sweat drips from the ceiling.

I was pretty well known inside because of my dancing and I definitely knew how to party. I attended DCM's every single Saturday from 2005 until it eventually shut its doors.

It was one of the roughest and seediest clubs around, but I wouldn't have had it any other way—it was all about drugs, alcohol, police, bikies and great NRG music. I made a lot of great friends there and I became mates with Neil, who realised I was no trouble—all I was about was having fun.

Neil was a giant man on the door. Every week he seemed to get bigger and bigger. He would sometimes crack little smiles here and there and if you were lucky you may get one. If you have been lucky enough to meet Neil, you would realise he was well respected by everyone. No-one would mess with Neil and everyone would respect what he had to say. He also has a heart of gold, but he sometimes hides that very well.

On the door, he followed rules and he was very fair. He would pick and choose the right group of people to walk into DCM's. Guys would react at times, but as soon as they did, they'd realised that Neil does not back down and they would back off. Neil would lay the rules down if you wanted to get into DCM's and if you didn't go by his rules you would know about it.

I've seen Neil in a couple of arguments, but never seen anyone have the balls to throw a punch, they all decide it's best to back off. From what I remember Neil was not scared of no-one. Neil made sure everyone who got into DCM's had a good time.

DCM's will always be remembered and will always be known as the best nightclub ever. If you asked anyone about DCM's the main two things they would bring up would be music and big Neil on the door.

Robbie Awad

PART ONE
THE NORTH

1

Primary School

My name is Neil Cummins. After reading this book you will get to know the real me. You'll share what I have been witness to and you'll feel the pain and the happiness I have been through. My story will give you an insight into my life for nearly 40 years, in the the underworld of two of the world's great cities, 15,000 miles apart. You'll find out what goes on in the dark corners of a pub or nightclub that the average person just wouldn't see. And you'll also find out why I was nicknamed The Muscle.

I was born in the freezing winter of January 1974 at Broadgreen Hospital in Liverpool in the north of England. My parents, Geoff and Carol Cummins, were in their early twenties. Both Liverpudlians born and bred, they worked hard. My dad was in the nightclub industry. My mum was a part-time model and worked at Broadgreen Hospital.

In the 18th century, Liverpool was one of the major ports in the world and brought in trade from all over Europe and the West Indies, including slaves. By the 19th century, Liverpool's dock land was massive, with a lot of West Indians settling in parts of the city, mostly around Toxteth.

The Muscle

Liverpool has one of England's oldest black communities and it is also home to one of the the oldest Chinese communities in Europe. The city has the biggest Anglican cathedral in the UK and the fifth largest in the world. Liverpool was also the port of registry for the *Titanic*.

But Liverpool is most famous nowadays for its music and its sports. On the music front, there is the Fab Four—the famous Beatles. Other bands and musicians to come out of the city are Frankie Goes to Hollywood and most recently Atomic Kitten.

In sport, Liverpool is the most successful city in the UK. The city is home to two of the biggest football teams—Liverpool and Everton—but I would have to say it's Liverpool Football Club that everyone knows. There is a saying between Liverpool supporters that it is really Liverpool and Liverpool reserves that are the two football teams in the city!

Boxing is also very popular in Liverpool and the city has a lot of successful homegrown talent in John Conteh, Andy Holligan and Robin Reid. And, of course, how can I forget Aintree racecourse? It is home to the most famous steeplechase in the world, the Grand National.

Before Margaret Thatcher came to power in 1979, Liverpool had been the heart of industry. Coal, steel, petrochemicals and shipbuilding—these industries made Britain and kept those around me employed. That is until Thatcher took an axe to them and sold off the big corporations. And when everyone scrambled for social security, she took an axe to that too. All the river cities of the north—the Mersey, Clyde, Tyne, Wear and Tees had massive unemployment. The dole office queues got longer as gradually all the docks became empty.

With all this unemployment, there was a rise in crime. It was an easy way of making fast money. People would rather sell drugs or do an armed hold-up than stand in a dole queue for hours. If you got caught you would get a slap on the wrist or a few years inside and before you knew it you were out and doing it all again. When Margaret Thatcher died, Liverpool didn't grieve; instead, lots of people held parties to celebrate.

When I was born, my parents and I lived at my grandparents' house for a while in Allerton. Then we moved to a little flat outside Liverpool to a place called Runcorn. I don't remember too much about Runcorn. The only memory I do have is having Christmas there and wearing a cowboy costume that I got as a present.

My parents owned their own place and they both had jobs, which was a lucky and rare thing for those times. Don't get me wrong, they weren't posh or fancy. My mum was a little though. But I think she just didn't like telling people she was from Liverpool because she didn't like to be called a scouser. This is what you're classed if you come from Liverpool— not a Liverpudlian but a scouser. It was a nickname given to us from the famous stew we make. Scousers were known to be rough and be dole lights (someone who lives on government pay-outs) as we didn't like to have a full-time job. We would earn our bread and butter another way. People from other cities were always told not to drive through Liverpool with their arm out the window as they were likely to lose anything expensive that they might have been wearing, like watches or jewelley. We are known to be the biggest thieves in the UK and the best at it too! Plus, scousers were known as party animals and piss-heads. Which isn't so bad. Every party needs a scouser to liven it up, I reckon.

The biggest thing about scousers is we don't take shit from anyone, no matter who you are. So that's why sometimes I know my mum wouldn't say she was from Liverpool. Whereas me and my dad are proud to say we are just that.

My dad was always busy, always working. He loved working in the nightclubs, and he was always coming home in the early hours of the morning. All the women in the area knew my dad: they would see him at the club or chat to him about how it was going. Most of them all went to the clubs that my dad ran. Mum wasn't too happy about all that female attention he got, but I think my dad liked it. He was a good-looking bloke. Can't blame him for that.

My mum was always restless, always looking for the next best thing. She wanted the best of everything. So the next thing was we moved to Widnes, about 10 minutes away from Runcorn, to a new housing estate. We bought a three-bedroom semi-detached house right next to Widnes power station. We would go there every weekend as it was being built and see how it was going. My mum designed it very stylishly for the time, but it would be retro now. The dining room had square wall mirrors and green leafy patterned wallpaper—but it was the late 1970s. The reason I remember that dining room so well was because I spent so much time in there. I could never leave the bloody dinner table until I had finished all my veggies. What kid likes brussels sprouts? But I have a lot of good memories of living there.

I had lots of friends in Widnes and I used to hang out with a few older kids playing football. I learned to ride a bike for the first time—the only thing was my dad didn't tell me when he had let go of the bloody bike and I panicked and rode straight into thorn bushes.

Got my first pet as a kid there too. My parents bought me a cat—I'm not sure why they bought me a cat because I wanted a dog. I think Mum wanted the cat. I remember being a brat one day to my mum. She had told me off and sent me to my room and she wouldn't let me go out and play with my friends. I was so upset that while I was in my room I opened my window and started yelling out at the top of my voice to all our neighbours that my mum was hitting me and asking them to help me. A neighbour came over to make sure everything was okay. It didn't get me out with my friends any quicker though.

Mum was a workaholic. She loved her work at the hospital, where she was like a clinician, giving needles to people with heart problems or doing blood transfusions. Sometimes she was called into work at night and, because Dad was out at the clubs, she took me with her. I liked going into work with her. While she was doing what she had to do, I would be in the office playing on all the machines or walking around the wards. I even got used to sleeping in hospital beds if I was tired. All the nurses knew me so I was never stopped from going anywhere, but the one place I loved to go was the operating theatre. I'd never seen a room like that before and the only time I had was on TV. I used to love watching the TV show *The Six Million Dollar Man*. I used to think that's where everyone got their own bionic arms and legs.

One night, Mum was called into the hospital to look after Bill Shankly. For anyone who doesn't know who he was, then shame on you! Shankly was the former Liverpool Football Club manager and a legend. When

Mum told me we were going into work and she was looking after him I was excited, but sad too as he was dying. Mum spent a couple of nights at his bedside where she said he would talk to her for ages. I wish I could have gone into the ward where he was, but I was never allowed—I really wasn't supposed to be there. Mum kept coming back to her office and kept me updated about him, knowing how much I was into my football and the football team.

My mum was so upset the morning Bill Shankly died. She had become close to him while he had been there. I was in shock with the news and kept thinking back to when John Lennon had been shot only nine months earlier. Even though I didn't know either of them personally and I was only a young kid, I felt like I really did know them—they were legends to me and my friends.

The city was still getting over the Toxteth riots that tore it apart thanks to the leadership of Prime Minister Margaret Thatcher. It left parts of Liverpool looking like a war zone. So with the death of Bill Shankly, the whole of Liverpool just went into depression again. I remember telling all the kids at school that my mum was looking after Bill Shankly while he was in hospital, but kids at that age think you make up stories to be better than them. They never believed me.

My family was comfortably well-off—not rich, but more comfortable than most of the other kids. Put it this way, we never went without anything and we could always get the best of everything. The only problem was that Dad was never at home at night. That pissed Mum off a lot, but I liked it as I got to see him during the day.

I sensed when things started changing between my parents. They were arguing a lot more and my dad just went out working more. Sometimes he didn't come home until the next day. I knew there was another woman my dad was seeing but being so young I just didn't pay attention to what was going on around me.

Dad took me to the house of the woman he was seeing in Aigburth, a posh area of Liverpool. I loved going to her house because she would spoil me with food while I was there. That always kept me quiet. She even came to watch me play football once. I just liked the fact that her sister was married to Graeme Souness, another well-known Liverpool footballer. He was sometimes there when we would go over. It's funny that even years after my dad stopped going around there, I would still look out for her as I was driving around or if I passed her house I would look to see if she was there.

Football is the first thing you learn as a kid in Liverpool. You live and die for football and your team. It's a part of everyone's life in the city. You couldn't get much higher in anyone's estimation, if you played football for either Liverpool or the rival club Everton. For some unknown reason to me, my dad supported Everton. My grandad (my dad's dad) supported Everton as well. I was always red and always will be. My whole bedroom was decked out in the red and white of Liverpool Football Club, with posters of players and flags and shirts. There was none of the Everton blue in my bedroom. The rivalry was massive between the two supporters and it would be like that in the schoolyard too. For nearly a whole month all the kids at my school who were Liverpool supporters would not talk or hang around with kids who were Everton fans. It got so bad that the teachers had to get involved and put a stop to it.

We visited my dad's parents, Nan and Grandad, a lot. They lived in Allerton. For some reason my mum didn't get on with them very well. She didn't really want much to do with them, so I'd just go there on my own with my dad. When it came time to decide what primary school to go to, Mum really wanted me to go to Carleton House, a private school in a posh area of Liverpool. Dad wanted me at the local primary school where he and his sister had gone. My nan had gone there as well. It was another opportunity for my parents to get into a big fight and for Dad to storm off and go to his club, where I think he felt at ease. Not that my mum couldn't hold her own. She had a temper too. She would push my dad's buttons and then I think he couldn't take it anymore. Even if I answered her back she would quickly tell me where to go as well.

I don't know how, but Mum got her own way on this one. So I started school at Carleton House. All the kids there were either from a rich family or their parents were famous in some way. A couple of kids had fathers who were Liverpool football players. There was one kid who's father, Tony

Malloy, was good friends with my dad. He was one of the main gangsters in Liverpool.

I didn't like it at Carleton House from the very beginning. I didn't really fit in and so I didn't make any really good friends. Still to this day I have no real memories of that school. I did win the egg and spoon race, and my dad won the parents' sports day. I got to hold hands with a girl and kiss her, but can't remember her name. Everything else is a big blur.

At the end of the second year at Carleton I really didn't want to go back. Apart from not having any friends, I was scared of the teacher who would be taking the class—just like everyone else in the school. She was a big woman, with dark hair and glasses. The rumours were that she loved to smack you over her knee with a ruler. We called her the Hitler of all teachers. I was really scared and kept complaining to my dad about it. He finally put his foot down and moved me to Springwood, a stone's throw away from my nan and grandad's house. He told me years later that one of my teachers at Carleton, Miss Andrews, had the hots for my dad and wanted him to take her out all the time. She would always turn up at my dad's club.

In 1980, around the age of six, I started at Springwood Primary School in Allerton, just down the road from Nan and Grandad's, Pauline and Chris Cummins, who lived nearby at 72 Redington Road. They had lived there since their house was built in 1913. My grandad worked at the local Ford factory making cars and then he took early retirement. Nan was a stay-at-home mum.

Allerton is mostly parks and it has heaps of sports fields and pubs. It also has the biggest cemetery in Liverpool. Allerton is famous for being featured in a lot of Beatles songs, like Penny Lane in Allerton Road and Strawberry Fields, which is at the back of Allerton golf course. Everyone in the area knew everyone and was very respectful of one another. All the people who lived in Nan and Grandad's street had been there since the houses were built.

We had a bit more money than the other kids, but I was never spoilt. Okay, my dad would buy me the latest sports shoes and football boots, but that was because I loved my sport. We went overseas a lot for holidays, to an island off the coast of Spain called Tenerife. It made some of the other kids jealous of me, as they could only go to North Wales to a Butlins Holiday Camp. I had a lifestyle that these kids had never seen before. I was never a show off, but come school holidays I would come back to school all tanned and the other kids would be wondering were the hell I had been. I got teased a lot at that age for being tanned, as I was the only kid who had a sun tan.

I loved Springwood school, I made some good friends there and they are still good friends to this day. The school was so close to my nan and grandad's house I practically lived with them. If Dad was there during the day I would stay there after school until late or until he had to go to work. Mum didn't seem to mind at all and I would stay there instead of going to the wards and waiting for her at the hospital. She knew how close I was to my nan and grandad.

I got into the habit of going there for lunch on school days as well, and Nan would be ready waiting to serve me a hot meal. I felt like I was in a restaurant. She really spoilt me, did my nan. On the way home, I'd throw the packed lunch my mum had made into the bin and would tell her I ate it all.

Lots of kids at Springwood school had parents who were out of a job. Their dads had been on the wharves or the docks, or they were working at the local Ford car factory, but got laid off. They'd see their dads at the betting shop or at the pubs or some were driving taxis to get by. A lot of dads had spare time but they didn't spend it with their kids, just with each other at the pub. Jobs were hard to find. But my dad was lucky and had his head screwed on. He was in the right industry and knew the right people. Everyone loved to go out to forget the tough times, and the pubs and clubs were booming. People would go out on a Friday and Saturday night and blow all their dole or wages until they next got paid. To them it was worth it.

I settled in very quickly at Springwood. When I first started there I was so advanced I was put a year above my age group. Then I was told I had to stay down another year as I was too young. Within a week of being there I remember being asked out by lots of girls in the year (we don't muck around in Liverpool when it comes to girls—we start young). I was asked out by one girl, her name was Sarah, and I went with her nearly all the way through my Springwood years.

One thing I did become famous for at Springwood was fainting. I lost count of how many times I would faint at assembly. I even fainted while doing the school play. I was playing Joseph and I fell off the stage and I was caught by one of the teachers. After that a teacher would always stand near me at assembly in case I fainted. I'm not even sure why that used to happen, but it got me off school for the day when it happened!

I loved every minute at Springwood. When I got to my last few years there I became the bell ringer for when there was a break or when it was lunch or home time. Sounds nerdy, but it got me out of class early.

Growing up, my best mate was Lee Burns. I became friends with him when I was six years old and at Springwood we were inseparable. We went everywhere together and he was like the brother I never had. His family took to me like their own and as I was an only child it felt like an instant family. I didn't mind being an only child as I had lots of friends, but sometimes I wonder what it might have been like if I did have a brother or sister. The other friends that stand out are the Springwood boys—Phillip Woods, Wayne Robson, Brian Wright.

I loved my sports as a kid and I always made sure that I wore the coolest sports stuff. I wanted the latest trainers from Adidas or Nike, the latest brand T-shirts and the best footy boots. My mum bought me some cheap T-shirts and sweaters from a shop that was just not cool to wear clothes from. So I cut out the Adidas and Fred Perry labels from some shirts and sweaters that were too small for me, or my dad didn't want anymore, and stitched them on the T-shirts my Mum bought me. Not one kid realised what I had done!

My hair back then was long, in a mullet like everyone else in the 1980s. We all wanted to look like the footballer Paul Walsh, who had the same hairstyle. My hair was curly as a kid and I hated that. So before school sometimes Dad would take me to the hairdressers and get them to blow-dry my hair straight. My mullet had style even if it's hard to think a mullet can look good. Yeah, yeah I can hear you all saying 'he was a pretty boy back then too'.

I soon got over straightening my hair every day for school. I got sick

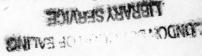

of maintaining the mullet and wanted a short back and sides. One night I was staying over at Nan's and I asked her if she would cut my hair. I told her what I wanted and sat down on the stool in the living room. I didn't think it would be too hard for my Nan to cut the mullet off and give me a good haircut.

Nan went to get the scissors and came back with a saucepan from the kitchen cupboard and put it on my head. I thought she was playing a joke on me, but before I could stop her she had taken out the scissors and was cutting my hair all along the sides of the saucepan. I was panicking, thinking I should have waited until after school to get it cut, but I trusted my nan would do a good job. I went to school the next day with the haircut from hell. I never asked my nan to cut my hair again.

My parents had met and started a family when they were quite young. They had some happy days, but most of the time it was just a lot of arguing. Mum was busy with her full-time work and it seemed, to me, to be her priority. She spent a lot of her time trying to get my dad out of the clubs. She didn't understand that the clubs were his whole life. And whenever she did talk to him about that he would get pissed off. They would fight all day and night sometimes. Mum would push my dad's buttons about staying out and all the women flirting with him while at the clubs. She would start losing it. Sometimes the arguing and the fighting was scary and when Dad would lose it I wanted to just leave. I was always in the middle of it all. I didn't ever want to take sides, but I just wanted to make the fighting stop. When they finally told me they were getting a divorce I didn't know at first who I would go and live with. I didn't want to choose one and then upset the other.

I knew my dad could cope living on his own and I thought my mum needed me. So when they asked me to choose, I said I'd move out with Mum. The house in Widnes was sold and Mum and I moved to a flat in Woolton in Liverpool. It was a nice place in a posh area of Woolton. We used to go there quiet a lot as my mum had a friend who lived on the same estate. The good thing was that we were even closer to my school and to my nan and grandad's place. Dad moved into Nan and Grandad's at Allerton for a while, which was better for him than moving out totally on his own. He wasn't ready to settle down and he never liked living that far out of Liverpool anyway.

I took it pretty hard at first and I was split between them. Sometimes at our new place in Woolton I would see Dad sitting outside the flat waiting to talk to Mum, but she didn't want to know. Sometimes my dad would break down in front of me. Most of my friends' parents were still together. I didn't want to talk about it to them so I tried to keep it quiet for as long as I could. When my friends found out they asked a lot of questions about my parents and I tried to palm them off so I didn't have to talk about it.

My dad was football mad. He loved playing it more than watching it. He started up a team in the early 1970s called All Souls, which was named after the local church in Allerton, and eventually became Allerton FC. Allerton had two football teams, one that played on a Saturday and one that played on a Sunday. Dad played for both. The Allerton Sunday team was better and had the best players. They played at Springwood Park, which was this massive park with one tree just smack bang on the side of the football pitch. They all used to use it as the team's changing room. The crowd that watched them was huge and wild. Other teams would shit themselves when they came to play against the Allerton.

Dad played for a number of teams on Saturdays—the ones that stand out are Mossley Hill and Aigburth People's Hall (A.P.H.) team. But he always played for Allerton on Sundays. The Allerton Sunday team won every trophy possible in the amateur Sunday league. The cupboard at Nan and Grandad's house had all his trophies—player of the year, player of the match or man of the match. He's won everything to do with football and out of all the amateur players that have played in Liverpool he was the most respected. I remember counting all his trophies once while I was still at school. I counted over 80 medals and trophies. Once he was even asked to play at Anfield, the home of Liverpool FC, for the Liverpool All-stars against an All-stars Celtic team, with the likes of Kenny Dalglish, Steve McMahon and many more ex-Liverpool players. To this day he still plays socially.

Dad was a health fanatic. Even though he worked in the clubs until late at night, he would have a few drinks socially but that was it. And he never smoked. Nearly every night after school, Dad and I would play football in the park and if we weren't playing football we would go running around the streets together to get fit. I wanted to be just like him in football. I have to take my hat off to my dad with his football. He was a very good player and could have been more than just a Sunday league player.

Dad always gave me stick for being a Liverpool fan and always tried to turn me to the blue side with Everton, but it was never going to happen. The closest he got me to the blue side was when he bought me an Everton strip, but that was only because I collected football strips. That was the situation all over Liverpool with families divided between the red and the blue of both teams, but it was a friendly rivalry. It was great to watch and listen to the rivalry when the game was on the television in the pub. No matter who won everyone was still mates after.

I started my football career at Mossley Hill, while my dad was playing for them on a Saturday. I signed for the under-11s as striker (centre forward). I scored 22 goals in my first season, but my dad secretly wanted me to play centre half (defender) like him. I studied my dad's form at the games to see how he played so I could copy him. I liked playing as a striker but Dad had a word in all my coaches' ears. 'You should be playing our Neil in defence, not up front'. All the bloody coaches would listen. I probably would have gone a lot further with my soccer career if I had listened to Dad's advice. Instead of trying to be the next Ian Rush or Paul Gascoigne, I should have been the next Alan Hansen. When I did finally listen to his advice it was too late in my career. And by that time I was too busy clubbing and partying every weekend!

So you can guess who my favourite teacher was at Springwood school —our sports teacher Mr Wells. I have to thank him for pushing me to do cross-country running. I was against doing it, but he kept on at me all the time to give it a go. So when I finally gave in to him I was selected for the school team. I didn't do very well in my first race. Coming 51st out of 70 kids running, but after training with my dad for a few weeks, when it came to my third race I came 10th. Then after that I was never out of the top three. When I was 10, I was the number one runner for the under-12s in cross-country in Liverpool. At one cross-country meeting in Stoke I had the chance to become the number one cross country runner in the whole of England. Dad was on the sidelines cheering me on. I was winning the race with about a mile to go when the steward of the race sent me the wrong way! The kid in second place was from the local school in Stoke and he took the lead. I looked back and saw my dad going off at the steward, shouting and grabbing the fella by the shirt and about to almost knock him out. I was devastated. Dad had trained me hard and it was like he was out there running himself. After that my dad was barred from coming to any of my races because he had grabbed the steward. After that I kind of lost interest. I carried on for a little while but that day killed me as I had worked so hard for that day.

All kids in my school wanted to grow up to be footballers. It was so hard to make it and get taken on by a professional club. If I was a kid now I reckon I would be signed up straight away. Anything to do with sport, my dad was there for me. He encouraged me out there for sport whenever he could, not pushing me but supporting me in whatever sport I was doing. He knew I loved anything to do with sport. Even in the summer we would play tennis twice a week, but it would be competive when we played.

I was obsessed with any sport, particularly football. Mum wasn't that interested in my sport. Once she did turn up to see me play football in a final. She had never come to watch me play before and I was really excited to see her there, but then at half time I looked around the ground to see her and she had gone. I don't think she realised how much my footy and my sports meant to me. Even when I got older and had trial after trial with football clubs and played in finals she never came to watch me.

Even though he was a great player, Dad was always injuring himself. I lost count of how many times he would break a bone or dislocate a body part—nose, foot, toes, fingers, ribs, arms and legs. Dad had more broken bones than former footballer Bryan Robson ever did because he was a hard tackler; he always wanted to win the ball and was good in the air.

Once he broke his leg and was on crutches for three months, but that didn't stop him from trying to keep fit and get back on to the footy field. Plus going to the Mossley Hill football club function and taking me along with him and walking home five miles to Nan and Grandad's house. He was still living with them so they dropped us off there in the car. When we left the function it was one o'clock in the morning and too late for them to come and pick us up again. Dad turned around to me and said 'let's walk home'. So we did, laughing together and playing knock and run on the houses as we went. I knew Dad couldn't get away fast because of the crutches, so he always got spotted. As soon as the cast came off he was running and kicking a ball around again. Dad was my best mate, we were like two peas in a pod. I missed my dad living at home, but I could see he was more relaxed now—he was more interactive with me and everyone around him.

After a few months Dad moved out from Nan and Grandad's and went to live up in Bradford, about two hours away, but I still got to see a lot of him. I went there for weekends or in the school holidays. He lived near the Yorkshire Moors, which was scary at night. We'd go for walks and even in broad daylight I was shit scared, thinking about all the dead bodies that were scattered all over the Moors but never found. At the time Dad was living up in Bradford there was a killer on the loose named the Yorkshire Ripper. Dad would always get stopped by people as they thought he was Peter Sutcliffe, as they apparently looked alike with dark hair and dark facial hair. My dad was glad when the Ripper was finally caught so people left him alone. He was also mistaken for Mark Lawrenson who played for Liverpool. Once, at a service station, a guy walked up to him and asked him for his autograph. Dad was a bit lost as to why he wanted it. When the guy realised he wasn't Mark Lawrenson we laughed. Now that was funny.

Maybe he was a bit lost, or maybe Dad was just over nightclubs I don't know, but Dad left the nightclubs and started selling cars and antiques, for about six or so months. He drove different cars every day, sometimes prestige ones. Once he picked me up from school in a Porsche 944. That was a really cool car. Back then not many people had one of those. I didn't mind Dad picking me up from school in those cars! Mum was just as bad, picking me up from school in her 1984 Mazda RX7, with the windows and sunroof down and the music blaring. So you can imagine what all the other kids in the school would start saying about me. The rumours went around the school about my parents and how much money and cars we had. One kid told the whole school that he had seen me and Dad get out of a helicopter. Like hell!

Soon enough, Dad was back in the club scene again, taking over a place called Ugly's on Duke Street in Liverpool. That place had an ugly face at the front of the venue for its sign. Most of the time I would just sit in the office when I was there or wait in the car for Dad to finish work. Dad reckons he worked with the hardest doorman there. Old Mikey and Tommy Bennett ran the door. They were both stocky, were both only five and half feet tall. Dad said they were terrifying when they fought. You knew when they meant business because they would put their black gloves on to sort people out. Once they cleaned up eight guys they knocked back on the door. Dad said it was all over in two minutes with all eight guys on the floor out cold. That was back in 1980. Dad had met my mum at Ugly's back in his younger days before Dad took it over.

It was nothing like Chauffeurs, the first club Dad had before Ugly's. Back then, Dad was working at the Ford factory with my grandad. Charlie Scott, the owner of Chauffeurs, talked Dad into running and being the licensee of the venue and leaving the factory at Ford. He jumped at the chance. Chauffeurs was big and had three levels. It was the first disco Liverpool had at the time, which made it very popular. It was a very posh venue for a nightclub back then; it was a place to be seen.

Charlie was a nice bloke—small and stocky with a hard face. Charlie was one of the guys who stopped the Kray brothers coming into Liverpool to get a piece of the action. Charlie, back in the day, was a hard man around Liverpool, someone you didn't mess with. He waited with a few other guys at Lime Street Station for the Krays to show up and when they did he told them they weren't welcome. Now the Kray Brothers (twins, Ronnie and Reggie) were among the most notorious gangsters in the East End of London and the UK at the time. You name it they had done it. They were ruthless, but that didn't stop Charlie. The Krays never came back.

Chauffeurs was where my dad got to know all the Liverpool and Everton players. They would come down to the club every weekend after they had played. Some of the Liverpool players, in particular Graeme Souness and Sammy Lee, both became very close friends with my dad. Football players like Tommy Smith and Jimmy Case were regulars at Chauffeurs as well. His brother Frank played football with Dad on a Sunday. Dad told me that he would always have to put Souness in a taxi at the end of the night, because he would be so drunk on champagne and he didn't want anyone to see him like that.

Chauffeurs was also the hang out for gangsters and coppers on the take. The Malloy family were the main gangsters back then—Jimmy, Tony and Kevin Malloy. They would usually do over warehouses and eventually Tony got eight years in 1974. They had one certain spot they would always sit at in the club. Jimmy Malloy was also doing a few jobs with another gangster called Tommy Smith (not the footballer) and they fell out over one job they did. Tommy came into the city looking for Jimmy and carrying a shotgun. He found Jimmy in Ugly's nightclub. Tommy shot the first round into the air and the second into Jimmy's leg. As he was leaving Tommy got stabbed and slashed.

The Vice Squad were regulars at Chauffeurs. They would often come down to find out what was happening and if anyone had any information on local crime. Most of the time they would also come to meet up with gangsters and to get payments from them. How do I know that? Because it was Dad who would give them the thick brown envelopes.

Chauffeurs was an amazing old building with lots of history behind it. Back in the day it was used by all the chauffeurs to drink and stay at while their masters did business in the city. It was a scary place if you were ever there by yourself, because it had so many rooms and the place was said to be haunted by one of the horse men. I had my fifth birthday there—that was cool with all my school friends and their parents arriving at the club. I remember that day like it was yesterday. I had big collars on my shirt and my birthday hat sat at the end of the table.

One day, while at Springwood school, Dad turned up to see my teacher and the headmaster. They called me out of class. I was thinking 'what have I done wrong?' The headmaster, Mr Wilson, said 'We are letting you go home early today Neil, as your dad has a surprise for you'. All I kept thinking was 'What's going on?' So when Dad told me that he was taking me to see all the Liverpool players at Anfield I had a smile on my face the size of the Mersey Tunnel.

We finally got to Anfield and I walked under the famous coat of arms, which you do just before you go on the pitch. It's there for all the Liverpool players to touch before they go on to the pitch to bring good luck and to put fear into the other team. Even though he was an Everton supporter, my dad didn't take me to Goodison, home of Everton Football Club. He knew I wouldn't go and wasn't interested in meeting their players. He knew I only wanted to go to Anfield, the home of my heroes.

It was hard to even get into the training ground and get a picture with a player, never mind going to their home ground to meet them all! I couldn't get the smile off my face. Everywhere I turned it was 'Wow!' For a kid who loved footy and supported Liverpool this was a massive moment for me. All the players greeted my dad as we arrived as if he was someone everyone knew. The players called out his name like he was one of the boys—'Hiya Geoff. Alright Geoff. Haven't seen you for ages. How are ya Geoff.' I sat in the players' lounge with all the players while they had their lunch and talked to them—as if we did it all the time! I even stole a chip from Graeme Souness' plate. Just sitting next to Alan Kennedy, Craig Johnston and Kenny Dalglish was a dream come true for me.

In the boardroom and the trophy room Dad said, 'Lift up the trophy Neil!' So I lifted up the trophies like the players do when they win. Lifting the European Cup over my shoulders was amazing. It was a wish any footy fan and player would love to do and I did it at 10 years old.

Dad said I could go out onto the pitch and I walked from one goal line to the other looking up at the stadium and at the Kop, the most famous section of the old Anfield stadium where all the fans would sing and chant their favourite player's name. I really wished one day I'd play on that pitch and score a goal. Then Phil Thompson came out on to the pitch and gave me his Liverpool number four shirt. I put it straight on and I still have that shirt to this day. The next day at school everyone came up to me asking what I did and who I'd met. Even the teachers were keen to know and wouldn't stop asking me questions.

At 11 years of age I had my first serious girlfriend. Her name was Sarah. We would hang out in the Springwood Park after school, go on a bus ride up to Allerton Road shops or go to the cinemas on a Saturday afternoon. We saw each other for 12 months. But just like a lot of girls, she preferred an older boy and called it off with me, just as we were going into secondary school.

About this time, my mum met Ray. Ray was a regular at Dad's new nightclub, the Club Continental, and they met there. Ironic, isn't it? Club Continental opened in 1981 and could hold up to 500 people. It was big and funky, and it was the place to be seen. All the footballers and gangsters went there to get noticed. Jan Mølby and Paul Walsh, both Liverpool players, went nearly every weekend. It's funny how Mum would go to the club my dad ran instead of going some place else. When Dad found out Mum and Ray were getting serious, he was really upset and angry. Dad spent a lot of time on his own and I tried to calm him down. It was really stressful and upsetting to see Dad like that.

Over the long summer holidays, my best friend Lee and I would hang out together in Allerton. I spent most of my time in Allerton instead of where I lived as all my school mates lived down that way. Plus it was where I felt more at home. We would get bored and look around for some trouble. Not that we would do anything bad. Dad had always told me to keep the Cummins name clean, and I never wanted anyone to put us down, so I always tried to cover up anything we got into trouble for. Despite this, Dad would always find out what I was up to. He was too well connected and everyone talked about everyone else, all the time. Even people I didn't know who, were Dad's friends would shout out to me: 'How are ya, young Cumo', but most of all it was respect to my nan and grandad as they had been in the area for years.

I didn't do that much with Mum, even though we lived together all through my childhood years. I would do my own thing at home in my room on the computer or play this football game I had called Subbuteo. I would play for hours and hours. Wish I had kept it as it's worth thousands now. I also loved to draw, which was one of my main hobbies as a kid.

Lee loved boxing, and wanted to be a pro boxer when he got older. We would sit around the shops and talk about how Lee would become middleweight champion of the world and I would be playing for Liverpool. His brothers all boxed, and Lee was starting to show his talents too. One day this lad called Paul Ellis, who lived near Lee, came walking down the road.

He thought he was a bit of a hard knock around the streets, and the way he walked down the street got to me and Lee. We thought he was a dickhead.

'Let's see if we can get a legger off him,' says Lee. So we shouted at him across the street, calling him names and giving him cheek, trying to get some reaction. Lee gave him the finger, while I shouted out the finger song, 'bend it, bend it, double it and send it' giving him one finger, then doubling it and then giving him two. Don't ask me why we used to do that! Just as I finished shouting the finger song, Ellis ran across the road after us. We legged it but as we were trying to jump a fence to get away from him he grabbed me and headbutted me. As he did that, my friggin' tooth fell out. With a mouth covered in blood I turned to Lee to see what we should do, but Lee was just standing there laughing. He always did that! Lee's brothers caught up with Ellis a few weeks later and had what we called a 'word' with him—he backed off after that. Since that day, me and Ellis have never spoken. Not even when I have come back for a holiday and I still see him in the pub. I fixed myself up at Lee's place and cleaned up so my mum wouldn't know and told her that my tooth fell out playing footy in the park. She would have completely lost it and would probably have blamed Dad for it.

2

Liverpool Nightlife

There's no another way to describe the nightlife in the northwest of Britain except to say it is full on. And there is full-on money to be made as well. Liverpool has a massive history of live music. The famous Cavern, an early club for bands in the 1960s, like the Beatles, is still pumping every night with live music.

People come from all over the UK and the world to visit Liverpool's clubland. It has been voted as having the best nightlife of any UK city, even beating London. Creamfields, one of the biggest dance festivals in the UK, is on there every August bank holiday. In the city centre, there are clubs on nearly every street corner—dance clubs, wine bars, pubs and some high-class restaurants that turn into nightclubs late at night. Everyone in Liverpool does the same thing when they go out on the weekend. They start off at a pub and then move on to a big nightclub until the early hours of the morning. Rain, hale and shine the clubs are packed. Everyone from 18 to 40 years old lives for the weekend, and most clubs stay open until 7am.

Liverpool Nightlife

People love clubbing because it's their way of relaxing after a hard week working, but other people go out because that's what they live for. Everyone wants to hang where their favorite celebrities hang out. People want to be seen in VIP booths. You can get freakshows, theme nights, light shows and lots of random stuff going on. Everyone gets really dressed up in their best clothes to go out—it's all about being seen. No matter what the weather, it could be pissing down raining or bloody snowing, girls will still go out in their little short dresses and high heels.

When all the ships left the Liverpool docks, they were empty for years. Huge spaces where people had worked just became ghost towns. There was a TV series about it in the 1980s, called *Boys from the Blackstuff*. The TV show was just like what life was really like back then in Liverpool, with a guy who was on the dole going around everywhere looking for a job, saying 'giz a job, I can do that', and if they would, he would give them the famous Liverpool kiss—a head butt!

We had other famous TV shows that made people see Liverpool in a different way—the likes of *Bread*, *Brookside* and more recently *Hollyoaks*. The Albert Dock area was completely revamped in the late 1980s with shops and cafés then later on with bars, restaurants and hotels. The biggest Garden Festival was built by the famous River Mersey just to get people to come back into the city and get Liverpool back on the map again. The city's Mathew Street Festival turned into the Liverpool International Music Festival held every year, attracting thousands of people. The atmosphere at the festival is massive. Pubs and clubs are packed day and night, with people even drinking and dancing out on the streets.

New clubs are always opening all around the city centre. The Buzz nightclub was like a rave club and The State nightclub on Dale Street was massive in its day and packed every weekend. The State nightclub was an old Victorian building transformed and gutted to be a dance venue. You couldn't go there straight—you had to be on some kind of pill or on a trip.

Chillies and then Chillies 2 were pumping, and there was also the more upmarket club called Streets and across the road was Bar One-11 on Hardman Street, which was the place to be seen. The Barcelona Bar had a nice name but even I thought it was a bit rough as it got a bad reputation for fights and shootings. The Krazyhouse was busy with backpackers. There was also Yates, Chibuka and Heebie Jeebies. Not forgetting Club 051 and one of the biggest gay clubs in the UK, called Garlands, which was a place a lot of celebrities would go to knowing they wouldn't be hassled there.

All the clubs played the latest dance tunes and the top hits. In the early 1980s, the biggest music on the dancefloor was disco. It was huge. I was like all the other kids—I loved chart music and I'm not afraid to admit I liked Billy Ocean, Fleetwood Mac, Stevie Winwood, all the 1980s hits. As an early teenager I was more into Bobby Brown and MC Hammer. I even thought I could dance like the Hammer. When I was a kid I used to pretend I was a radio dic jockey, playing and mixing the music in my bedroom. It's funny how I can look back on when I used to go clubbing to now and see how things have changed. Like the way we dance at clubs. Back then, everyone would dance doing the side step and the girls would dance around their handbags on the floor. Even I used to do the running man dance thinking I was Vanilla Ice. Now everyone dances to the DJ or they just bounce up and down, going off their heads.

Charlie knew everyone and if you needed something done, he knew who to get to do it. I would sometimes go with Dad to Charlie's house when they had to meet about the clubs. When we got there, Charlie would grab me and shove me into his broom cupboard until they finished talking. I'm still not sure if he did that because he didn't want me to listen in on their stuff or he did it for a joke—either way I hated it. It was pitch-black in there and I was crammed in with brooms, suitcases and mops. He would lock the door and I couldn't get out.

After a few times of this, I told Dad I'd wait in the car. Charlie would come to his front door and tease me saying that he was going to come and get me. Do you know a funny thing? Charlie is my godfather. I know my mum never wanted that.

My dad wouldn't go looking for trouble, but he can look after himself if need be. He was licensee of a small club in town, which you had to enter by going underground. For the life of me I can't remember what the name of the club was. One night he came over to my mum's house in Woolton with his face covered in bruises with a broken nose. I listened in on my parents' conversation as Dad described how two guys had come into the club before closing time and hid. When everyone had gone home, my dad was alone adding up the night's takings. Suddenly they ran out and bashed him up badly. Then they locked him in the big safe he had on site and ran off with all the money.

Mum started yelling at him saying 'What the hell are you doing in the clubs' and going off, but Dad just said 'It's my life'. It was a bit like old times. The word got around the streets of what had happened to Dad. After a couple of weeks the guys were caught and dealt with by certain people who knew Dad and the thieves were sorted out privately. That was the way we did things. Things got sorted out a lot quicker if you did it that way rather than going to the police. Once word got out someone would buckle, knowing that they had picked the wrong person or club to do over. In 1987, my dad was asked if he could change sixteen thousand pounds from a post office job done by a few local gangsters. They had used too much jelly to blow the safe and nearly all the notes had been peppered. To change the money, Dad had to get someone to write down all the notes that didn't get peppered. Who did he get to do that for him? My nan. She saved ten thousand of the peppered notes. Didn't think my nan had it in her. Go Nan!

Another club Dad was licensee for was the massive Club Continental, which opened in 1981, and Dad was there until 1985. When the club closed down, the famous Cream nightclub took it over. The clubbing scene took off with Cream in the 1990s and it brought so many new people to the city. People could see how good the nightlife was in Liverpool. Even the top DJs wanted to keep coming back.

After the Club Continental, Dad took over a wine bar/restaurant outside the city centre in West Derby called Porterhouse. It was an opportunity for him to be part-owner. Plus it was another chance to get back into the club scene again after taking a break from it. It was a cool kind of place where people went to for food and drinks after work. I worked there on weekends and in the school holidays to help out, stacking bottles in the fridge and cleaning the cellars. Dad saved a lot of money on cleaners having me there! But I don't think it was really Dad's kind of club. Plus the area was mostly all pubs and it wasn't really an area for a wine bar/restaurant, even though Dad's friends would always come down every weekend.

I never paid much attention to who my dad had meetings with or who he was meeting at the cafés we would go to. If Dad was meeting someone, he'd just ask me what I wanted to eat and drink, and that was it. The guys he would meet would always say to me, 'How are you, young Neil' or 'Young Neil, are you going to follow in your dad's footsteps?' They would always spoil me while I was at the café. I remember that the people would usually wear black leather jackets and they all reminded me of gangsters from the movies. There was even one guy, with a shaved head, who had a massive scar on his face—I certainly remember him.

Nightlife in a city like Liverpool brings out everyone, especially the 'top heads' as we called them—dealers and gangs. Sometimes when you were out you had to be careful not to let anyone know where you were from. If you said you were from Allerton, and then a gang from Speke turned up, it would all kick off into a big fight. Gangs called for back up and they'd be waiting outside the pub or club for you if you tried to leave. There were even certain places in Liverpool you couldn't go to if you were from Allerton and if you did, you had to make sure that you were invited to that pub by someone who was known in that area.

My dad never talked about the people he hung around with at the clubs with or who he was in partnership with. He was private and respectful in that way. Now I've worked in the industry myself, I know all the types of people that my dad would have dealt with every day. But he always held his head high, kept his mouth shut and held his nerve. It's something that I learnt how to do by watching him with these guys and gaining their respect. I would watch the way my dad talked to people and presented himself. I don't know anyone who has a bad word to say about my dad. I know a lot of people in Liverpool would love my dad to be in business with them or even run their business for them.

Dad keeps a lot of things to himself. Maybe it runs in our family. My grandad didn't open up about his life or his emotions either, he kept it all to himself. It took him 40 years to talk to me and anyone in our family about what he did in World War II. For years, he told me he was just a cook.

Then one day, I was asking him again why he was constantly scratching his leg. Had he been bitten by something? He suddenly opened up and told me it was from the war, from walking in the swamps in the jungle carrying the big machine guns. He told me that for days on end he would be in water up to his waist, along with snakes and leeches. Some nights they had to sleep standing up in the swamp. He talked about the Japanese men he had shot. He explained how terrified you were of walking on a mine field and the worst was when he saw guys he had become friends with die or get shot or even lose limbs. He hadn't been a cook at all. Grandad received the Burma Cross for what he did in World War II, which he gave to me before he passed away. Why did he scratch his leg, you ask? He had lots of blood clots and skin rashes from the jungle.

When I was about 15 years old, Dad became the licensee and manager of another of Charlie's nightclubs called Le Bateau in the city centre. It was a funky kind of club for people over 30 and became legendary in the club scene. Bands like the Supremes, the Strokes and Talking Heads played there. It was in a thin terrace, sandwiched between two buildings. There was a wine bar with a restaurant upstairs and a nightclub downstairs. I thought that nightclub was so cool and so did a few girls at school who heard that Dad had a club in Duke Street. It had dark timber furnishings and downstairs there were heaps of glass mirrors. Disco balls were making a big hit then and every club had to have one.

As long as Lee and I looked like we were 18 we could get into clubs without an official ID, because you didn't need to show any and no-one had one. Even your driver's licence didn't have a photo on it. Even though I had a baby face, I was tall, which got me in. Lee was broad and had a hard face which helped him as well. I remember the first time I went to Le Bateau with Lee, the doorman stopped us.

'Not tonight fellas.'

'But I'm here to see Geoff.' As I said that, he had a smirk on his face to say you don't know who Geoff is.

'Who are you?' he asked

'I'm Neil, his son.' The doorman didn't believe me so he went and got my dad who came the front door not expecting it to be me. When he finally came the door Dad's jaw dropped and even the doorman's did too. I remember my dad saying to me 'What the bloody hell you doing here?'

'I'm going out.' He couldn't believe it. He asked where I was going.

'Hippodrome or Fridays.' Even when I walked in with Lee, Charlie was at the end of the bar and he yelled out, 'Young Cummins, what you doing out.' We had a few drinks with Dad and Charlie, and then we left. A few of the barmaids wanted to come out with us until Dad told them I was only 15 years old. I think the barmaids thought they were in with a chance.

Dad kept a lot of his club stuff at my nan and grandad's place. I came across his stack of free invites and passes for Le Bateau and thought, 'Hey I can give these out at school to some of my mates and to girls, which will make me look really good!' The next day I gave out about 100 of the passes to my friends, and did that for the next few months. A lot of kids from my school got into the club using them and some of the girls I gave them to passed some on to their mothers. I even gave my art teacher a pass once, not that it got me a better mark! I never told Dad about this! I wonder if he knew? I became more popular with the girls who were older than me. The club closed in 2012, but it's just reopened in 2013 to be one of the biggest student bars in Liverpool, but Charlie doesn't have it anymore.

3

High School

I am a Liverpool FC fan through and through. Kenny Dalglish, former Liverpool FC player and later manager, was my idol, a legend, a great person and a family man. Ian Rush, another Liverpool player, broke every record and was probably the best striker in the league back then. Before they used to show live games on the television, I would be in my bedroom listening to the game live on the radio and then watch the highlights on television.

Liverpool FC has had its share of historic moments, both on the pitch and off it. In 1985, I was visiting my Aunt in Wales, waiting for the European Cup final between Liverpool and Juventus at Heysel to start, when a report came over the TV that the game had been postponed and abandoned. All the players were coming out on to the ground to calm down the fans. There was actually a riot in the stadium. Italian fans had run at the Liverpool fans and the Liverpool fans had run back at them, making the wall collapse, killing 39 Juventus fans. It didn't give Liveprool FC fans a good name and Italy wasn't a place you wanted to go on a holiday if you were from Liverpool that's for sure. Liverpool was barred from playing in

Europe for six years after that.

But it didn't stop me from following the team. I would even bunk off school and get a bus to all the way to Melwood, where Liverpool Football Club had their training ground, and climb the walls to watch them. Better than doing history lessons. I would watch the whole three-hour training session and then go and wait by the main gates to the training ground and get everyone's autographs.

When I was 11, I left Springwood Primary School for New Heys Comprehensive School. Still just a stone's throw away from my nan's.

At Springwood, I'd been popular and I reckoned I had most things under control—my footy, running and girls. At New Heys I was out of my comfort zone. It was bigger, with older and tougher kids. Many of the kids had a reputation for being 'hard knocks' around the area. I was cool at Springwood—but I didn't feel so cool now. There were kids at this school all the way from Dingle, Speke, Wavertree and even Halewood, all known hard places of Liverpool.

There were all sorts of rumours about New Heys, that all the new kids had their money stolen or, if you didn't hand your money over, you would get a ciggy stubbed out on your face, or that you had to do jobs for the older kids and if you didn't, you got beaten up. As I walked into the schoolyard I could see that everyone was staying in tight groups from their own suburbs. I quickly found all the Springwood boys. All the boys that came from Springwood all met up by the main gates. There were a few faces I recognised from playing against them in footy for Springwood.

On my first day, the head teacher, Mr Leeson, pulled me aside.

'Are you Geoff Cummins' son?'

'Yes, sir.'

'When your dad was here he was a pleasure to teach. I hope you'll be just like him.'

No pressure! I knew he'd be keeping an eye on me. So every time I had Mr Leeson for a lesson I would always get on with my work and not mess around in front of him. I didn't want to disrespect my dad. Mr Leeson was a good teacher and I enjoyed his classes anyway. I have a lot of respect for him. He was firm but good and would always give me advice if needed.

High School

There were a couple of rough kids, one was called Mark Kelly and the other was called Mousey. Kelly was from Garston and he was a so-called 'top head', someone who thinks they are a bit of a tough nut. Kelly had a reputation for fighting and kids said he had once bitten off someone's ear in a fight. Both of them kind of bullied the new kids who came to the school. They never tried it on with me or any of my friends, but I did see it happen to a few other kids in my year. It's funny how now, when I see people like that who had this hard reputation at school, I look at them as if they are nothing, but I think that's more down to how I have changed. I was like my dad, I wouldn't go looking for fights, but I wouldn't shy away if I had to.

My mate Lee was like my brother. Everyone knew Lee and the Burns family. They were my second family. His brothers were at the same school and they looked out for us. Lee's brothers were well-known boxers throughout England and had a tough reputation around Allerton. Nearly every weekend one of them would end up fighting someone in a pub or club. Lee and his brothers hated Kelly and Mousey and got into a lot of fights with them over the years. Once Lee wanted to knock out Kelly, so they met at Garston Park to have a scrap. Lee didn't win that one, but he showed he was willing to have a go no matter who it was, and that he wasn't scared of anyone. Lee was a great street fighter. If he could have fought in a boxing ring like he did on the street, he could have made it big in boxing.

Mum and I were still living in Woolton. All the boys in that area knew me and they all hated the school I went to, as they all went to Gateacre Comprehensive. There was a big rivalry between schools—a lot of kids would meet up for fights at parks. I was the new kid in the area, but I didn't go to their school and they didn't like that. I had a bit of a reputation there for not backing down from people if they wanted to have a go and I was very protective of my friends. Some of the kids there were jealous of me as some of the girls in the area were asking me out. I started seeing a girl called Gillian from Gateacre Comprehensive and I would go and meet her outside her school gates after school. I think that's why I would get into fights a lot around there, as I would turn up in my New Heys uniform to meet her.

The Muscle

When I started to get into fights, I began to realise my own strength and what I could do with my body. Mark Jamison was the first guy I seriously hit. He had been on my nerves all day at school and everybody had been egging us on to have a fight. When we were changing classes, I stopped him and we started arguing. One thing led to another and I hit him in the face. I knocked him over the hedge he was standing by and split his jaw. He went down and I walked off. I was proud of my punch. The next day we were friends again, typical of the kids back then. He gave me respect after that. I felt real good about it. It got me a lot of respect in the school. I knew I could hit and hit hard. I would never hit punching bags as a teenager, because I thought it never really showed how hard you could hit. So I would practice hitting timber fences or walls, even metal or brick walls at one point. I would hit it as hard as I could for three minutes in a way that I would damage the wall I was hitting to the point it would snap or dint. With the bricks I would see if I could get one loose from hitting it. It sounds weird, but it was effective.

In Woolton, I had a friend that I had been mates with for a few years called Jonathan. Both our mums had been friends for years. Before I moved there I would go to his place and hang out with him. It made it easier to settle in when we moved. Jonathan told everyone in his school not to mess with him anymore or else he would get me to deal with them! He would also tell everyone I was his cousin. One day after school he knocked on my door and said that one of the tough boys from his school called Dorgie was picking on him. All my mates know that I'm very loyal and if anyone picks on them, I am the first to deal with it. So I went to Dorgie's home and knocked on the door. His mother answered it. I asked if Dorgie was home and she told me she would go and get him. As he came to the door I just knocked him clean out before he had a chance to say anything. 'Don't mess with me or any of my mates okay', I said, 'and leave Jonathan alone. After that everyone one in the area gave me respect. He talked it up sometimes, but if I ever found out that he was mouthing off I would just turn up at his school and confront him. He soon buckled.

The reason why I did get a lot of respect was that I sorted out shit by myself and didn't bring down four or five mates to do it with me. If anyone ever did try to put it on me while I was by myself and they were with their mates. It would only be a matter of time until I caught up with them when they were by themselves.

In Allerton, there was a football stadium for a team called South Liverpool, a small club which used to be the breeder for the likes of Liverpool Football Club, bringing in talented players. In the school holidays or after school we jumped the fence and played footy in there. We would play footy all day in there if it was a nice day and sometimes we put the flood lights on as we knew where the switch was, but that meant the bizzies (police) usually turned up and got us all out. They would drive past and see the floodlights on and think, 'Hang on a minute no-one plays there anymore, so why are the bloody lights on?'

We all loved playing footy there, sometimes so many people from the area would turn up it would be like 16 on 16 sometimes—I loved the place and the old stadium had a lot of history behind it. A lot of famous players had played there and it was one of the oldest clubs in England. I remember just before they closed the ground Liverpool reserves played there against South Liverpool in a cup match. Liverpool had a few first grade team players playing that night. Even I played there twice for my Sunday team, Mossley Hill. It was brilliant. Not long after the ground closed some kids jumped the fence at night just to hang out and smoke ciggies or pot in the stands and they burnt down the whole bloody stand, dressing rooms and all. After that it was bulldozed. I saw the lad who did it down at the shops and I couldn't believe that he thought nothing of it. He didn't care at all. I hated him for that. That was a piece of history gone, but you only think like that if you're madly into football.

I would train nearly every night for football and for my match with Mossley Hill, which we played every Sunday. My dad was playing for the men's team on a Saturday. Mr Deitz, my sports teacher, was really important in my life. He pushed me with my football and helped me in any way he could. He played footy against my dad and became good friends with him. I really wanted to be a football star. My problem was I always wanted to be a striker, when everyone else could see I should be playing in defence. Dad never pushed me, but he supported me to get on and encouraged me to succeed. There are not many bad things I can say about Dad at that time. We never had any big arguments when I was growing up as a kid. Football was our life. I just wish I had made it for him.

Me and my mate Tommy got tickets to the 1989 FA Cup semi-final match between Liverpool and Nottingham Forest at Hillsbrough, which was Sheffield Wednesday's ground. Tommy didn't want to go. As we had been going to a lot of away games to watch Liverpool all season, we thought if they get to the final we would go to that instead. So we gave our tickets away.

Instead we went into the city centre to do a bit of shopping. While we were heading back home on the bus, we listened in to the footy on a fellow passenger's radio. But we couldn't believe what we were listening to as a tragedy started to unfold. Some of the Liverpool fans were trapped at the front of the stand against a fence. People kept pushing their way in through a tunnel that led into the stadium. But there was such a huge influx of people trying to get in through the tunnel, that it had caused a massive crush at the front, killing 96 people and injuring hundreds more. As the events of that tragic moment, now known as the Hillsborough disaster, came through on the radio we were gob-smacked. All we kept saying was we should have been there too. When we got to Tommy's house we turned on the TV. A couple of days later we found one of our mates from Allerton two years below me was crushed. He also used to play for Mossley Hill FC.

The whole of Liverpool was affected—everyone knew somebody who had been killed. At the end of the day was it worth it for a football game? A lot of people stopped going to games after that. Even me and Tommy stopped going for a while—and Mum always gave me a hard time if I talked about going. It hurt the Liverpool FC a lot—another tragedy after Heysel. They held a lot of counselling sessions for everyone. Me and Tommy skived off school to go to Anfield and put our scarves on the ground in respect. There were heaps of wreaths, flowers and shirts and scarves left there by people. It was a site that will forever stick in mind. Words can't describe what Anfield looked like on that day and how all supporters of every football team came together to show their support.

Not long after this, my dad lost one of his best mates, Eddie. Eddie lived above a record shop in Penny Lane, the famous street that the Beatles wrote a song about. The 'shelter in the middle of the roundabout', the barber shop and possibly the bank (whose banker 'never wears a mac') mentioned in the song are all on Smithdown Place, which is at the junction of Allerton Road, Penny Lane and Smithdown Road.

Eddie was a nice bloke. He would always would sit at the coffee shop outside the record shop having a coffee. He was always smiling and he reminded me of Burt Reynolds, the actor. Dad was always hanging out with Eddie and we would go around to Eddie's place at least twice a week. I liked going around there because Liverpool schoolboys football ground was to the side of his flat. I watched them from his window as they were training. I would play there too when I was older.

One day, Dad went round to see Eddie. He knocked on the door and there was no answer. This was typical, so as usual Dad went around the back of his flat to get in. When he got to the back he saw that Eddie's garage door was open and Dad looked in. There was Eddie, crushed underneath his car. He had been working on his car when the jack holding part of the car up had broken and the car had fallen on top of him. Dad rushed in but it was too late, he had been dead for a while.

This devastated my dad. He was in shock for months and he never talked about it again. Only sometimes would someone mention Eddie from Penny Lane, but Dad never talked about the day he found him. Even when writing this book and bringing Eddie up. I could hear the delight in my dad's voice to talk about his mate and to know that I still remembered his best mate.

Even though I lived in Woolton with Mum, I spent as much time as I could at Nan and Grandad's. I wagged off school to go to their place, just telling them that I had a free period from school. They would believe me as they didn't have a clue. I would sometimes tell them there was a teachers' strike to which my nan would say 'again'. I got my nan to write me letters sometimes so I could have the day off, pretending I was sick so I didn't have to go to class. The good thing about this was my mum would never find out, as my nan didn't talk to her. I would go shopping with them sometimes and when they went shopping the dog came too, as Grandad would walk the dog around outside while me and my nan would shop. That's my grandad for you, he loved all the dogs he's had. He would take the dog for a walk and take it past all the schools so the kids could stroke the dog. He'd also take a pocketful of dog biscuits to feed his dog and any other dogs that they came across on their walk. The bloody dog would come back from its walk fatter than when it left. It got embarrassing when he would still come past my school when I was 15 years old, asking my mates, 'Have you seen Neil? Because Sam the dog wanted to say hello to him.' Can you imgine what my mates would be saying?

Nan and Grandad loved gardening—well, my nan did. She would get my grandad digging and planting every day when he just wanted to sit down and watch the horse-racing on TV. Everything is buried in that garden— four dogs and two budgies, plus about 20 of Grandad's war medals from when Dad buried them in the back garden, when he was a kid, and forgot where he put them, never to be found.

My grandparents taught me a lot. They taught me to respect your elders and even taught me to cook and bake cakes. To this day, I still cook certain things the way Nan taught me to. I never wanted to let them down. I always tried to make sure they never found out about any trouble I got into. Even now I still think what they would say if they knew half the stuff I have done. Later on, when I went out clubbing with my mates, I used to tell my grandad that I didn't drink alcohol, just to keep him happy. My grandad was never a drinker and he thought that people who drink were trouble-makers. So I would say me and Lee were going out for an orange juice or we were going to play pool, but really we were going clubbing. Even now, if I do something I shouldn't, I feel they are watching me.

When I was about 15, I helped Dad out at his club, often to cash up in the mornings. We would be there for four to five hours, sometimes with me skipping school to go there with him. I always found something to do, like pretending to be a DJ, or counting the small coins—all the old two pence pieces! Once I counted 200 pounds worth and then I found out that all he wanted it for was decoration in the office! Most of the time I would get to post things for him, which I didn't mind because the post office was at the other end of town.

High School

One of the funniest things happened once while I was at New Heys. A kid in my class called Michael was a pretty crazy kid. He asked a few of us if we fancied having the day off school. We looked at him 'Nah not today' as we thought he meant to bunk off, but he meant for the whole school to have the day off. We said 'How?' He said he would get everybody the day off tomorrow. We thought he was a bit weird, so we didn't take much notice. The next day, Michael didn't turn up to school so we didn't think much of it. Suddenly at 10am the school alarms went off and fire engines and police raced over to the school. The teachers ran around outside the school buildings like crazy. Our teacher told us we all had to leave the building quickly. No-one knew what was going on until we got outside and were told there was a bomb in the building. Michael had called the police from a telephone box from his street and told them there was a bomb in the school which would go off at midday. We were all sent home and as the police searched the whole school. In the end, Michael told the police that there was no bomb and that he just did it to get his mates the day off school. A legend, but a dickhead at the same time.

As we grew up, Lee and I were inseparable. We went everywhere together, including on a holiday to Majorca, off the coast of Spain when we were only 14. We were the life of the party, cracking jokes, making people laugh, drinking and partying wherever we went. We were scousers, and everyone knows a scouser is the life of the party. Everyone in the hotel we stayed at loved us, girls included. Guys, girls and even older guys were knocking on our hotel door asking us to come party with them or to hang with them by the pool. I even had three girls who were staying at the hotel, but didn't know each other, ask me out. Two of them were 16! While there I met two guys who I would play football with for Hereford, two years later.

Even though we were only 14, we got into every nightclub. We had a fight in a bar there with a group of four or five guys who were about 20 years old. Two 14-year-old boys taking on 20-year-old guys in a bar? That was me and Lee! We beat two of them inside the club, but they had more mates outside and we were outnumbered. The fight happened all because we tried to pick up the girls they were with.

'Neil leg it, there's too many of them,' shouted Lee. We copped a bit of a bashing but we walked away with our heads held high, knowing we gave it to them as well. Lee and I thought we were famous even before we were. We reckoned that we could get any girl that we wanted and we could knock anybody out if they started a fight.

Most kids hung out in their local areas in Liverpool, at the shops or on the estates. It was a territory thing. About 10 to 15 of us hung out at the Cress—the Crescent shops on the border of Allerton and Garston. There wasn't much else for us to do. After school, we'd have our tea and watch *Neighbours* and *Home and Away* on the TV. None of us would meet up until those two shows had finished. Then we hung out at the shops until about 10 at night. I would usually stay at my nan and grandad's if I was hanging out. Then when I got a little older I would ride my mountain bike home. We messed around and perved on girls from different schools. Sometimes we went on a bus or train for a ride into the city and back. Sometimes kids would steal cars and do drive-bys at the shops to show off. One guy was putting on a show, but lost control and drove straight into the bus stop getting chased by the bizzies (cops). He got out and legged it. He was lucky. Sometimes someone would buy cans of beer from the off-licence and we'd drink them at the shops. We would drink Carling Black Label. It was cheap, but it was strong. Usually that would be on a Friday night with no school the next day. I remember one time we all stayed over at this lad's house while his parents were away. We all got someone to get us lager, vodka and wine from the off-licence. We were mixing our drinks and one by one we all got so pissed that we all started throwing up everywhere. When we woke up in the morning the place was a mess. His uncle cleaned the place up and also went off at him. We would also play knock and run on people's houses, let bangers (fireworks) off in people's letterboxes, throw eggs at cars and house windows, and sometimes water bombs. We even used to super glue all the letterboxes together on people's houses. Yep, typical teenagers.

One night we threw eggs at a police van as they drove past. Suddenly they did a u-turn and all of us ran in different directions. I ran to South Liverpool's ground and onto the railway tracks. I could see more cops ariving, so I hid in thorn bushes for an hour and a half and I could hear the police dogs—I just kept thinking what's my nan going to say if I get caught? What's my mum going to say, she'll go off her head! I stayed hiding in the bushes and holding my breath until they went. When I jumped into all the thorn bushes I ripped my new ski jacket to shreds. Only bloody got the jacket the week before. When I heard the police leaving. I ran back to Lee's to get my bike. He was already back there. And all Lee did was laugh at me and my ripped jacket. I threw the jacket away on my way home so Mum never knew. Only one of the boys got caught that night.

It wasn't just guys up at the Cress though. Girls would hang there with us as well. The girls who hung out with us could fight if need be. The girls wouldn't miss out on any of the action if there was any, throwing bottles instead of punches. Sometimes girls from the other gangs would turn up and the girls would show off and try to fight like the guys, but they mostly hung out with us because either one or two of them fancied one of us. So they would make all their friends hang out with us.

A lot of girls wanted to go out with me in New Heys, but I turned them down. Still to this day I say to myself what was I thinking turning them all down! There were some hot girls asking me out, girls that all the lads in the school would jump at the chance to go out with. I think I was shy with a lot of the girls and amazed they had asked me out.

I'd always wonder why they wanted to go out with me! Why, I have no idea! I was nervous about some of the guys they had been out with before they asked me. These guys were sometimes older by two or three years and they were well known through out school. I did have an on-and-off with a girl called Angela, but it never seem to work. We got on better when we weren't together. In the end I preferred girls from different schools and started seeing this girl from an all girls school in Woolton. Much better!

Joy rides in stolen cars were popular with the gang at the Cress. All the latest models would get stolen and the kids would put on a show around the shops for everyone. Then they would go and burn it in the park. I remember this one time we all went up to the golf course to watch one of the boys who stole a car take it for a joy ride over the greens and the sand bunkers. He lost it on the fifth hole after getting airborne over a sand bunker and spun it. He was okay. We just legged it once he got out of the car. A lot of kids were smoking pot or joints then and, because there were so many parks around, a lot of kids picked magic mushrooms as well. In summer you would see heaps of pot-heads in Springwood park picking mushrooms and listening to their Walkmans, most of the time with Pink Floyd playing. There weren't a lot of junkies then, even though heroin was starting to come around. It was mostly pot and E's. A lot of kids smoked from the age of 12. Smoking just didn't interest me. I used to hate it if I was seeing a girl and she smoked. I couldn't handle it and I didn't care how hot she was I would stop seeing her. I didn't like smoky breath.

Lee and me were really into our sports, so we didn't mess with drugs as teenagers. Mostly we drank cans of beer. I tried to be different and drink Bacardi and Coke, as that's what Dad drank and it was the only drink I knew of. It got me pissed quicker that's for sure. Lee didn't think boxers should use steroids and I wanted to keep fit for football. There used to be a lad who lived near Lee who was on steroids at the age of 16. He just looked wrong and with his body still growing his back was hunched. We didn't even smoke cigarettes. Lee and I were like that—a bit different to the rest. By the time most of us were 15, we'd had sex with a girl, but Lee and I weren't different about that. By the time lots of kids were 16 or 17 they were into running drugs for gangs to get cash. A few of them did armed hold-ups. That was the typical thing. I remembr this lad called Ryan from Speke, who was two years older than me. He did an armed hold up at the post office in Garston. For his getaway, Ryan hijacked a bus full of people because his getaway driver panicked when he saw bizzies drive past where he was parked. Ryan gave himself up when the bizzies gave chase.

The big thing back then was selling knock off clothes and sports wear. There was always someone selling the latest tracksuits or latest sports shoes. I used to have new tracksuits every week and all the latest sports shoes. One of the boys who hung around with us at the Cress started selling pot and as soon as he did that he changed. He became someone who thought he was all that and better than everyone else, thinking he was one of the big boys now. I just thought he was a dickhead.

When I was 15, my mum, Ray and me moved again—this time from

Woolton to Huyton. Mum was looking for the next best thing again and this time it was a bigger house. Ray had moved in at Woolton and so he moved with us to the new place. When I first met him he tried to get into my good books by buying me stuff and I knew he would keep doing this. But I was still distant because I didn't want to betray my dad. It took me a while to accept Ray. He owned fruit and veg shops around Anfield and Woolton. Sometimes he gave me a job working in the Woolton shop after school and Saturday mornings, which meant some extra pocket money.

Our move to Huyton was into my mum's dream house—a big house with a massive garden at the back with a huge fish pond and a long driveway at the front, with fern trees going the length of the drive-way both sides. It was impressive. It didn't bother my mum that I was out of my friend zone. She wanted this house and I must admit I liked living there. We had a garden at last and I liked gardening. My bedroom was massive, plus the house had two living rooms and we put a gym in another room. I had my own space; I miss that house.

Huyton was even further away from my school and my mates. It also was a rough area in places, just like Allerton. If you weren't a local kid who had come from there, you weren't welcome. I didn't get much trouble from anyone around there, but then again I spent as little time there as I could. I was still an Allerton kid, and took the bus down to Allerton to get to school and then stayed there. I'd take the bus to Woolton and from there I would get off and walk the rest of the way to Allerton or I took a mountain bike I bought. It took about 45 minutes, but I got really fit.

I felt embarrassed about my mother's big house. Don't get me wrong I loved it, but I knew how all my mates lived. All my mates lived in small, semi-detached houses and I didn't want them to feel uncomfortable if they visited me. So I never asked them over. About that time she and Ray started their own family and had two little girls. At first I didn't like the idea of having a sister or brother. I had enjoyed being the only kid, but after a while I didn't mind it and I looked after them sometimes when Mum and Ray went out.

Mum bought me a Great Dane dog—but we only owned it for half an hour before we gave it back. It was massive—it looked good and it sat on the lounge. But when Ray told it to get off, the dog stood up and growled at him. Even Ray shit himself—it was like Terminator. He somehow got it into car and drove it straight back to the owner.

A couple of days later Ray picked out another dog, a Rottweiler puppy, who I called Duke. I loved that dog. I'd hang out with him at home in the backyard and teach him tricks. Whenever the birds would fly into the back garden and try to eat his food I would shout 'birds'. Duke soon got the idea. Every time I shouted 'birds' that was his cue to chase them out of the yard. He hated them.

I walked Duke all the way to Allerton to show him off to my mates. They loved him. My mate Wayne wanted to come and see my house in Huyton. I tried to stop him from coming—I didn't want my mates to be jealous of me or anything. But he came up one night out of the blue, so I said 'Let's take Duke for a walk.' We walked down to the local shop to get some food. A group of about five boys came up to us, and suddenly without saying anything, one of them king hit Wayne in the face. Wayne went down on the ground, holding his head. They ran off, without giving us or even Duke a chance to do anything back. Wayne got up, and he was alright. We needed to get back at them.

'A lot of kids hang out at the sports centre. Let's see if they're there.

Wayne was all for it. 'If they're there, let the dog on 'em Neil!'

We got to the sports centre and could see them sitting by the tennis courts on benches. I shouted over at them. They looked over and stood up. 'Hey!' shouted Wayne to the boy who had king hit him. 'Come on! Do you want a go?'

Two of them ran, leaving just three standing. They were up for it. We starting walking slowly towards them, and when I was about 10 yards away, I shouted 'birds'. Duke went crazy. He was barking and frothing at the mouth, and straining at the end of the lead. The boys were terrified and ran off, but we didn't let them get away for nothing. We caught one of them, dragged him into the tennis courts and bashed him. I never saw them in my area again after that.

The problem was the next day at school Wayne told everyone about my house and everything we had—the latest computer, the latest clothes.

My friends all lived in houses like my grandparents, a block of terraces—some of them owned their houses but they were much cheaper. Mum had matched the furniture off the TV show *Dallas* that everyone was watching. We all loved JR. Mum wore big shoulder pads on her jackets and big jewellery.

Wayne told everyone that me and my family were posh. I decided I would never ask mates to my house again with them teasing me for what I had. I didn't need that shit.

4

Smack City

Outside London, Manchester and Liverpool are Britain's number one centres for organised crime.

In the 1980s, Liverpool was tagged by the media as 'Smack City' or 'Skag City' after organised gang crime and heroin trade exploded, especially in the city's more down-and-out areas. A lot of the gangsters fought for the control of the nightclubs. They'd buy into a security firm, which meant they controlled the nightclub doors.

Whoever had control of the doors had the power to say who could go in and sell drugs to the punters, and who couldn't. There were a lot of conflicts over territory and control of the doors between gangs who controlled drugs and nightclub doors. They would use a lot of violence to control the drug trade at their venue. You would get gangs bringing in the drugs to sell to the punters and the doorman would try to stop it by kicking them out or refusing them entry. But the doorman would be led off to one side and told that they will be done over if they tried to stop the dealing. That just didn't mean they would be slapped around a bit. The gangs would find out were they lived or even if they had kids. They would turn up at their school to show they meant business with this warning. The gangs evenually pushed out the doormen who were no good to them and brought in their own heavies.

A nightclub that was near Lime Street Station got a visit by a gang of around 20 guys. The doormen got told that all of them were out of a job and that they were taking over the door. They were told to keep their mouth shut or they would be dealt with. From what my dad said the doormen didn't get paid enough to argue and just walked away.

Most of the bouncers in Liverpool pubs and nightclubs when I was growing up were from what I call the 'old school'. They were mostly 40-year-old blokes who had been around the club scene for years. They'd often done time in prison, and they knew all the old-time gangsters and dealers and were usually ex-boxers as well.

For boxers working the doors, it generally meant the end of their career. They just couldn't resist the extra cash the gangsters were throwing around, and then before they knew it they were tied up in the underworld.

The gangsters would always try to get the up-and-coming boxers in the area to work for them. First they'd turn up to watch them and get to know them. Then they'd sponsor them at fights, take them out for dinners and clubs, flash a bit of cash around. Suddenly the boxer was hooked on the support and working for them on the doors. They'd let the gangsters in so they could sell their drugs to the club patrons, and they'd stop other dealers from coming in at the same time. They were paid good cash to keep the doors open for the gangsters, but they often paid the price for it, serving time in jail, taking the rap for the dealer they were working for, or getting shot by the competition to get them out of the way.

Most of the underworld uses doormen to control things for them on the streets and to be their eyes and ears in the clubs while they're not around. Some bouncers just liked to make a name for themselves and get a tough reputation, but most did it just for the money. Cash is always useful. Even young kids would work for the gangsters, thinking it's cool getting just 20 pounds to be a delivery boy. You looked good to your mates.

Britain's biggest drug-dealing cartel in the 1970s was called the Liverpool Mafia. They became one of the most powerful and richest gangs in the

UK. Liverpool Mafia protected its power base by its close links to the IRA and having a contract killing outfit called the Cleaners. They are believed to have assassinated more than 20 drug dealers around Liverpool. When the Liverpool Mafia started networking overseas one good friendship they developed was with the Cali cartel from South America. Some of the biggest gangsters became good friends with the Cali cartel, including Colin 'Smigger' Smith and his mate and business partner Curtis Warren. In 1995, there were close to a hundred shootings and several murders in Liverpool alone all over territory, control and power, between gangs who controlled drugs and nightclub doors. It got so out of hand that the Liverpool Police became the first in the country to openly carry weapons against the turf war.

Curtis Warren was one of the most famous and well-known bouncer-turned-gangsters to come out of Liverpool. He was a very stocky guy, with a presence about him. He was known as Cocky or the King of Coke by the media. With a personal fortune of over 200 million pounds in 2005 he made it into the *Sunday Times* rich list. Curtis has paid the price by going to prison for years, but he is the only person who really made a name for himself and made millions of pounds. He would study the dealers coming and going from the venues while being a bouncer on the door he worked at and how the drugs were moved and who moved them. He used his brain and wanted to go it alone. He wasn't bought off by getting maybe an extra two hundred pounds in his pocket. He planned to have his own drug runners, while he stayed standing on the doors. That's what made him successful for years, working under the radar while looking like a normal bouncer doing his job.

My dad first met Curtis when he was only 15 years old. Dad was working on the door of Chauffeurs, when this young kid came running up trying to get into the club. He was stopped by Dad and a doorman, but it turned out to be Curtis Warren trying to get away from the cops after trying to steal a car down the road from the club. The cops weren't far behind him and took him away. All his life he has been in and out of prison, for assault, armed robbery and drug trafficking. On 24 October 1996, Warren's villa he owned in the Netherlands was raided. Warren and several associates were arrested, with police finding three guns, ammunition, hand grenades, crates with gas canisters, 400 kilograms of cocaine, 1,500 kilograms of cannabis resin, 60 kilograms of heroin, 50 kilograms of ecstasy and 400,000 Dutch guilders, plus 600,000 US dollars in cash. The whole haul was estimated to be worth £125 million. He was sentanced to 12 years in prison. When released Warren was found guilty for conspiracy to smuggle cannabis. He was sentenced on 2009 to 13 years imprisonment.

Colin Smith's family lived down the road from my nan and grandad in Allerton. There was John, Colin and Kevin Smith. John Smith senior was the mastermind behind a lot of the drug trade in the 1970s, mostly importing them from Argentina. He paid off a lot of dockers and custom officers to get his shipments into the country and opened up the drug importing channels for others to follow. He never seemed to have much time for his kids or much to do with them. But it seems that whatever time he did spend with them, they learnt the family 'trade' quickly.

Colin 'Smigger' Smith was one of the biggest underworld names in Liverpool and probably the whole of the UK. The media portrayed Colin as the Scouse Cocaine King, but I just knew him as Smigger, my dad's mate. Like every other footy-mad boy, Colin would be down at Springwood Park every weekend watching his local footy team, Allerton, play on a Saturday or Sunday. He went to New Heys Comprehensive School (High School) just like me. When he was at New Heys he would sell a bit of weed to make money and look where it eventually got him. Colin was just a normal bloke to us. He was one of the boys, a family man, going down the pub with the lads and watching the footy. He was a mad football supporter, and switched from his local team, Allerton, to Everton Football Club.

Colin was 'Smigger' to his mates and a husband and dad to his family. I always remember as a young kid walking past his house near my nan and grandad's. He would be cleaning his car or walking back from the shops and would shout out to me, 'Alright, young Cummo?'. Cummo was my nickname from everyone who knew my dad. I never said much or stopped to chat. I would just say, 'alright', and keep walking. I was like that with everyone really. I kept to myself, unless you wanted to talk about football.

Everyone knew Colin and his family were people not to mess with, everyone knew he had money and was a good at business. Colin and his brother John once put money into the Allerton footy team, even though it was just a Sunday league team. Allerton had no stadium, and the players just played on Garston Park, but they didn't care, it was their local team. The Smiths signed the best players from other clubs, brought in players who were playing at a higher level, with ex-professional players signing for them, and even put players on wages. It was all just to make Allerton stand out as a team and as an area.

In 2004, my dad went into business with Colin and John with clubs and restaurants/bars. Dad was in partnership in a club called Soho Bar in Seel Street in Liverpool. It wasn't doing too well and then all of a sudden Dad's business partner did a runner with the money and left my dad with a big headache. At the time, Colin Smith was living in Spain and while my dad was over there on holiday he caught up with him and told him what had happened. The following week my dad got a call from Colin to come back over to Spain to Porta Banus were Colin lived at the time. Colin put an offer to my dad saying he would buy the bar, but he would demolish it and start fresh with it and keep my dad as a partner in it. He then gave my dad a bag of money to start the building work on the bar. When my dad got back to his villa and counted it, he had 112, 000 pounds—my dad, the highest paid janitor in the world. Colin was never seen and would just get people to drop off bags of money to keep the building going. The bar was renamed Above & Below, which could hold around 100 people.

In 2007, Smigger was asked to come down to a gym in Speke for a special event that was happening there. It was the re-launch of the gym that Colin had helped do up, putting in 20,000 pounds of his own money. From what I was told, he didn't really want to go. He couldn't be bothered, but he went as his life-long friend Robbie Hughes was begging him to turn up. Robbie Hughes was well known in the Allerton and Garston area. He had played footy with my dad for 14 years with Allerton. When Colin got there he was given a white T-shirt to wear with some writing on the back, something to do with the gym.

He said a few hellos to people. Not long after arriving there, his mobile phone rang. He had to take the call outside the gym as the music was too loud. As he stepped outside, the door was slammed shut on him. Still wearing the T-shirt, which was just as good as wearing a bullseye, he was shot twice from five yards away with a shotgun. He was dead before he hit the ground. Who set him up? Which mate asked him to come down to the gym and betrayed him, you ask. At the same time this happened a fishing boat was leaving Morocco bound for Southern Spain. On board was one million pounds worth of drugs, with a street value of five million pounds. Colin had put up the money for it, but Colin's business partners didn't want to pay Colin back so Colin was shot. An hour after the boat had sailed and five miles off the coast of Spain the boat started to take in water. Within minutes it started to sink, the people on board had no choice, but to send an SOS to the coast guards. In doing so they threw all the drugs overboard as they were weighing the boat down and they had to get rid of it before the coast guard and police arrived. All the drugs sank into sea. So Colin was killed for nothing in the end.

Dad called me the next day and he was devastated. He'd been hit hard by what had happened. Colin had been his friend, his mate. He was also close to his brothers and his family. Dad told me that Colin had asked him that week to come to the gym and train with him. Who knows what would have happened if my dad had gone and trained with him that night? I don't even want to think about it. It hit me hard for a few weeks thinking about it. I'd known Colin for so long. No matter what he did for a living, no-one deserves to die like that.

The hit was from close range using a pump-action shotgun. Even by the standards of normal gangland executions, this was ruthless and you can imagine how much mess the gun made pointing at his head and stomach. That killing sent shock waves through the underworld. Rumours flew around—nobody knew who did it. Colin was rumoured to be worth over 200 million pounds. Some said he was gunned down by the Colombian mafia, the Cali cartel. That would make Smigger one of Britain's biggest underworld figures to be killed on British soil and the first time by a Colombian cartel. I think that's all media bullshit—I reckon he was set up. There were a lot of jealous people in Speke and in the circle of friends Smigger had. One of the families Colin had a feud with was the Walls family, known throughout Speke and Liverpool as a boxing family. I knew

The Muscle

Colin Wall as a kid. He was always at the same boxing events as my mate Lee. As I am writing this, Colin Wall is looking at 15 years in jail, as he got caught with 800,000 pounds worth of drugs on him.

I think it will be years before we find out what really happened and who organised the killing of Smigger. Karma will come to that person or persons who dogged him.

Colin's brother, John Smith, was known as a hard man around the city of Liverpool, and his reputation was that he didn't take any shit from anyone. Out of the Smith brothers, he was the one you didn't want to fuck with. John had grown up in Allerton, and played and supported the same team we did, Allerton.

John masterminded shipments of coke to be brought in to the UK from Holland. He used to get a gang together to pose as 'booze cruisers', people who only went to Europe to get cheap grog on the passenger ferries that went across to Holland. But they brought back coke.

The police watched them for months. Every two weeks they brought in shipments of heroin and cocaine from Holland, without realising they were being watched. All the drugs were packed into cases of bottled beer and a ferry worker would then take them off the ferry past the customs official.

In 2006, they were caught trying to import 10 million pounds of class A drugs. John got seven years. The courts want John to pay 600,000 pounds back for 'illgotten gains' and accused John of moving large lump sums of cash from his UK bank accounts out to Spain where he owns houses in Marbella.

Dad visits John in jail twice a month. People say John and Colin weren't that close, but blood is thicker than water. When John does get out, the person or people who gunned down his brother Colin better find a good place to hide. Dad went into business with John with restaurant/bars and in the Jalons winebar in Wavertree. My dad even got a villa next to John's villa in Costa Del Sol.

Another family in the underworld when I lived in Liverpool in the 1990s was the Ungi family. David Ungi would watch my mate Lee boxing at the local ring or at the gym and sometimes have a go himself. In 1995, David and his family went to a pub called Cheers on Aigburth Road, Aigburth. John Phillips was on the door and stopped him from coming in. There was a fight, and David won, which some people said he only did because he used a knuckleduster. Phillips was apparently very cut up about it.

Later, David was driving in Dingle when a black car pulled in front of him and a man jumped out firing an automatic weapon. David tried to escape the bullets. It wasn't the first time that his car had been sprayed with gunfire. This time he was unlucky and was hit twice by the bullets, killing him instantly.

After David was gunned down, a big turf war started around the city. The pub that John Phillips owned burnt down and there were riots in Dingle where David Ungi was from, just 10 minutes from Allerton. Cars were burnt and there were lots of drive-by shootings. It took a while for things to calm down in that area. No-one has ever been convicted of David's murder. To this day no-one really knows the reason for the hit and they can't ask John Phillips, as he died from a heart attack.

David's brother, Ian, was known in Liverpool as a drug dealer and a hard man. Ian took over the reins of the business after David's death. He also owned a few bars and pubs, and bought one, a few years after David was killed, in Aigburth called Low Bar. Ian had a few enemies in Liverpool—which underworld figure didn't? His pubs were often being attacked. Daniel Smith and Jason Fitzgibbon, from Halewood, were major underworld drug dealers who didn't get on with the Ungis. A fight broke out between Ian Ungi and Smith, leaving Ian slashed and needing 72 stitches after being slashed with a Stanley knife. No-one was ever arrested for it, as none of the doormen, the only witnesses, wanted to give a statement as they feared for their own safety.

Michael Ungi was David's son. He tried to be just like his dad and take over where his dad had left off. This made him a number one target with rival gangs, and in around 2009 he was shot at in a drive-by shooting. A bakery shop that he owns near Allerton Road in Liverpool was raided by the police, suspecting he was selling class A drugs from the shop. It's reported that the drugs were placed inside the bread and sold to the buyers without anyone knowing. Unknown to them an undercover police officer bought a loaf of bread with class A drug inside. The shop was closed down. From what I was told he sold bloody good multigrain bread too.

James 'Pancake' Taylor is another well-known drug dealer, gangster and standover man. James was Britain's most wanted man until July 2013 when he was arrested at gun-point for an assualt and ambush on former boxer Lee Siner, who is another person I knew growing up. After Colin Smith was killed, Pancake tried to take over the drug trade in Spain. Pancake was rough and had a 'take no shit' attitude, who had got into the big-time from dealings with Colin. The only problem is that he was a so-called 'scallie'. A nickname for a no good scouser. He would never be as big as Smith, as Colin was old-school and his word mattered. People would listen to Colin as payments were always up-front and on time. Pancake had no social skills and the first thing he thought of was violence, then doing good business and getting respect.

Desmond Bayliss worked on the doors at The Arena and Modo nightclubs and was heavily involved in the cannabis drug trade. He was tried and convicted for a cannabis farm outside Liverpool along with 10 others. Police uncovered 800 cannabis plants and 1,600 empty buckets ready for drug cultivation.

There were some doormen around at the time that had become well-known gangsters. Bahman Faraji was well known for years for working the doors in Liverpool in the late 1980s and 1990s. His nickname was Batman, probably because he had a face you wouldn't forget, with a scar running down one side. He had a reputation as a standover man, which made him a lot of enemies. He didn't care who you were and he didn't respect anyone's turf. Faraji was a regular in my dad"s bar in Spain and would sometimes try to get work, but Dad always turned him down. He always thought he was untouchable but in February 2011, Faraji was shot dead at point-blank range outside a pub in Aigburth. My dad was one of the last people to see him alive, at a café days before his death.

Kevin Maguire and Nathan Jones were best mates and worked at the same nightclub together in the 1990s. In October 1998, they were both gunned down as they were leaving a gym. The killing was a contract hit about drug supply. It was rumoured that the killer carefully watched their every movement for weeks before the hit, even getting to know them in the gym and doing workouts next to them, before killing them. There were rumours that the hitman got 50,000 pounds for the killings.

Steve Bristow was an up-and-coming professional heavyweight boxer in the 1990s—he had everything going for him. He boxed for England and I would watch him at the same time I would go and watch Lee box at the Garston boxing gym or contests at Everton Park Arena.

Bristow started working the doors around Liverpool and then started mixing with the wrong crowd, making easy money. One night in 2001, the rivals of the people he was associated with turned up at the Streets nightclub where he worked and shot him five times. He nearly died, just scraping through to tell the tale, but losing one eye in the process. After that he always wore a bulletproof vest on the door. He threw his boxing career away just for a bit more cash. But a lot of doorman are like that—they throw away their success just for more cash in their pockets.

5

Liverpool Gangland

All the gangs in Liverpool did their business in the pubs. The gangs knew each other's territory. You had the Allerton crew, the Garston crew, then the Speke, the Wavertree and then Halewood gangs. I was with the Allerton Crew. We would hang out at the Cresent or the youth centre just next to the shops, but I was never officially in a gang. The gangs went out looking for trouble, I just looked after what was ours in our territory. Our mates would look for shit in Garston, stealing and beating up other kids, but Lee and I would go off and do something else. They were okay with that. They knew we wouldn't let them down if trouble came to our area. I just wasn't into stealing cars or doing someone over because they were from another area. There had to be a reason for me to do someone over.

Allerton Pub was where all the underworld people of our area would meet up. When the coppers found out about any deals going down, the gang members moved to another pub for their meetings, and then after a while they'd move back again. The Allerton Pub was packed on Saturday and Sunday when the football was on. If you walked into the pub on those days every corner of the pub would be taken by some top head doing some

Me and my nan (Pauline Cummins).

Me at five years old with a bad haircut.

Grandad, Nan and Sam the dog.

Dad and me.

My nan and me, at 12 years old, in my New Heys uniform.

A cheeky grin—seven years old.

My dog Duke and me at 15 years old in Huyton, Liverpool.

With my best mate Lee (on the left) on holiday in Spain.

Craig Johnston and me at Anfield.

*Surprise trip to Anfield, pictured with
the European Cup and League Cup.*

Doorman 'Bulldog' Franky from Chillies nightclub in Liverpool.

The Allerton crew at the Allerton pub for the funeral of the dog mascot.

Colin Smith's home off the south tip of Spain.

Jimmy Booth, standover man for Colin Smith.

Me and my dad at his restaurant in Allerton Road.

With my grandad and dad when I was back in the UK on holiday, after moving to Australia.

Money, money, money—my dad.

My dad's footy team, APH, after winning the league and Cup double.

Ray Burns, me and Paul Burns at Chillies nightclub.

With good friend Firass Dirani (pictured left).

Looking after Ja Rule while he was in the Cross.

With good mate Samoan Dave. He is second in charge of Notorious motorcycle club.

deal or sorting out a job to be done on someone. Watching the Allerton team play on a weekend was routine for everyone who lived in the area and then, after the game, everyone went the Allerton Pub until it closed. On those days if you weren't from Allerton, you just wouldn't go in. Even if you were with friends, you were playing with your life if you went in there and if you started something in there, then the only way out was by ambulance.

There was another side to the Allerton Pub. The Allerton football team mascot was a dog who went everywhere with the team. It even had its own bed in the pub while its owner Les had a drink with the boys. It was at every game, celebrating with a pint in its bowl after the team had won the cup. Someone would usually give it some speed and then everyone laughed as it chased its tale for hours. The only thing missing was the dog dancing on its back legs. When the dog died, aged 14, everyone gave the dog a good send off and buried it in the backyard of the pub. The dog had a white coffin, with flowers on top and two people carrying the coffin. Even the local priest turned up, along with the whole community, and we let off fireworks at the back of the pub. The whole area came down to the pub that night.

You could get anything at the pub. You could get drugs, hitmen, gang bashings, or just clothes and fancy goods. Everybody wanted cheap stuff and there were plenty of people who could get it for you. You'd just look for the skinheads with the tracksuits on or even the old blokes with beer bellies propping up the bar—if you needed something, they'd get it for you quick smart. They were also the people you didn't fuck with. When I was young, I wondered how these people spent every day doing nothing but still had money to spend? I didn't know then that they were part of the various gangs who would do things like hijacking semitrailers and lorries on the motorways. The gangsters of Allerton were big on doing those jobs up and down the country. In the pubs, you could get involved in some duty-free products coming into the UK on the cheap under the noses of customs. Another guy could get you any designer brand clothing you wanted. There would always be someone in the local pub trying to offer and offload something to someone. The main man for this was Micky

Boyle. He had connections everywhere.

In the UK, the shonky people wear brand baseball caps like Nike or Adidas, a Nike polo top, a pair of tracksuit pants and a pair of white runners. In Australia, it's exactly the same. There must be a shonky person website where they all buy their clothes from online! They stand out a mile away. If I was a copper I'd know who to pull over straight away.

The Speke skinheads didn't like anyone who came from Allerton or Garston, and vice versa. Lee and I had to go up to Speke to meet up with one of Lee's mates who he boxed with. As soon as we got there we knew we were unwelcome. All the local boys were watching our every move. It was like one of those cowboy movies where someone new in town walks into a bar and everything goes quiet. If we went to the bar, all heads and eyes followed us. They had all heard about Lee and his brothers, and Lee's attitude was, if they start something then we start back. I was Lee's minder that day, watching his back to see if anyone was going to start something. If we hadn't been meeting up with Lee's mate from Speke, who knew everyone there, we would have clashed with a lot of people that day. Even when we left, Lee's mate walked us out just in case we were followed.

Speke's gangland criminal network is largely under the control of one well-known family, the Walls. They have a big reputation in Speke and are usually the final word in any disputes or problems. Some of the little gangs of young lads from Speke aren't just violent though, they can be racist too and Speke is a predominantly white area. People don't go to the police around there though. If they do they're branded a grass and it can make life difficult.

Wavertree was the place everyone went to before going on to the city centre to go clubbing. Fights happened quickly with people who weren't from there, and Lee and I found ourselves slowly getting barred from a few pubs. I asked Lee to meet me at a pub in Wavertree on a Saturday night. I told him to meet me at about nine at the Clock pub. By the time I got there at 9.15pm he had already been fighting and told to leave. In that 15 minutes he didn't even get a beer in and the locals had started on him. I couldn't believe it. Everyone knew he and his family were boxers and were often in the paper. Paul Burns was the most well-known and even went to the Olympics for boxing as a middleweight and then when he got back he turned professional. Ray Burns was also a good boxer at the time, but he was like Lee: got into too many fights in pubs and clubs. When Lee was around, lots of guys would start a fight with him to see if they could make a name for themselves so they could boast that they could 'knock out a Burns'. I can tell you it never happened, and they never did. But that was Lee—he never shied away from a fight, especially when he had had a few. It got so bad in the end that Lee stopped clubbing in the city centre and just stayed local for going out so he could stay out of trouble.

The good thing for me was that when I went to the pubs, no-one knew me. Only the doormen or people in the club industry knew me through my dad. When Lee and I were at Chillies 2 in the city, Lee picked up a girl who was someone's ex. They weren't happy about it. As we left the club, we were suddenly surrounded by these guys ready for a fight. We were outnumbered, but three of the doorman knew who I was and came over and stopped it. If they hadn't, it would have been all over, red rover for us that night. It was good knowing a lot of doormen around the city at different venues. It got us into all the venues free and we never had to line up on the doors. A lot of them would let the managers know that I was Geoff Cummins' son and I was looked after.

Sometimes, gangs like the African guys who lived around Toxteth would come to Allerton or maybe to Speke, but they only came when they were looking for someone. There's a lot of guys in that gang that I wouldn't want to mess with! They were big guys, over six foot. They had a lot of territory and lot of backing. They would turn up outside a nightclub in the city, looking for a mole who had been ripping them off or someone dealing on their turf. One night at Club 051 they all turned up because they knew their mole was inside, because they had sent one of their boys in to see if he turned up. It was like something out of a movie. A load of cars rolled up and parked outside the nightclub waiting for the guy to come out. They were all suited up in their leather jackets standing across the road from the club. The only thing they did respect was that it had nothing to do with the nightclub or the owners of the club. That's why they didn't storm the place. Plus they knew who part-owned it and didn't want to make trouble with that family. A few of them tried to get in by putting it on the doormen but it wasn't going to happen. So they waited to do the business on the other side of the road. It was heavy; they were never afraid to use weapons in public if need be. After an hour waiting they were told he had left before they had got there.

Tony Richardson is a perfect example from gangland Liverpool. In 2007, he was known throughout the West Derby area of Liverpool, but lived in the Grizedale estate in Everton, north Liverpool, which on the outside comes across as a pleasant place to live. There are neat rows of terraced two-storey houses, there's hardly any graffiti and the cars that people own cost a lot of money. The estate sits in one of the most deprived areas in Britain, and was at the heart of a vicious gang war which left at least three men dead and dozens of others wounded. More than 250 of Grizedale's residents—around one in eight of the estate's population—have been arrested for drugs, weapons or violence. Hundreds of weapons were recovered from the estate including a powerful sniper rifle complete with telescopic sight and ammunition. Despite this, shootings and car bombings continued, and local politicians criticised police tactics and said that the situation was 'out of control'.

The feud between drug gangs in Everton and their rivals in Kirkdale had been simmering for years. Tony Richardson, whose fiancée is actress Jennifer Ellison, recent winner of ITV's *Hell's Kitchen* reality program, is something of a local legend. He was wrongly accused of taking part in a gun attack on a prominent local family linked to the Kirkdale gang. He was arrested and held in custody for four months before the case was dropped—in other words, he snitched. There is said to be a 50,000 pound contract on his head. As *The Sun* newspaper reported, 'An underworld source in Liverpool warned: Everybody now knows Tony's a grass. It is the worst crime. Any gangster would forgive you sleeping with his wife before he'd forgive a grass.' Then Tony Richardson's home was sprayed with gunfire during a drive-by shooting.

A few days after the attack on Richardson's home, a massive car bomb blew up outside Club 051 in Liverpool's city centre, smashing glass in windows in nearby hotels, shops and offices. Six days later a nailbomb was thrown into the middle of the packed Dickie Lewis pub in Kirkdale. The device landed inside the pub and even though it had been lit it didn't detonate. Police have little doubt that if the bomb, filled with razor-sharp shards of metal, had exploded the damage and cost to lives would have been massive. Tony was later jailed for eight years after a violent attack on boxer, Lee Siner.

Liverpool hardcore gangsters were people you just didn't mess with. They didn't care who you were, or who you thought you were. They'd just end your life in a split second if they chose to, whoever was around. What did they look like and how could you pick them out? It's hard to say. In Australia you can generally pick the people involved in the underworld – they are either bikies or gangmembers, often pumped up with steroids with tattoos all over them. In Liverpool, they look like everyone else, like skinheads, or just normal Joe Bloggs. Often it's not the big bloke you want to watch for, it's the skinny one who will usually be the toughest. The main gangsters try not to be noticed or to make too much noise, unlike the wannabes.

Lots of ex-professional footballers players were involved with the underworld and became drug runners or involved in protection. Mark Ward played for West Ham United, Manchester City and Everton. Once his career had finished, he went back to Liverpool and was taken in by the underworld. Finally he was arrested in Prescot on Merseyside in 2005 with 4kg of heroin and jailed for eight years. Some people reckon it wouldn't have happened to him if he had stayed south in London. The problem with a lot of professional footballers is that when they are out and about they meet a lot of people and those people are usually the local gangsters. They spoil footballers even if they don't need spoiling, party with them and take them for dinners to expensive restaurants, letting them use villas or boats that they may have overseas. Once they start to take advantage of the spoils, then the gangster owns them.

There is always rivalry between Allerton and Garston, and it came to a head one Saturday afternoon. All the gang leaders got together in Garston Park, which separates the two areas, to sort out the shit. It was a massive turnout, with people all ready to have a go at each other carrying baseball bats, timber, planks, metal bars and knuckledusters. It ended in a massive blood bath, all in broad daylight, while families and kids were in the park. Scousers are a funny bunch. A few weeks later people who were involved in that brawl were drinking together in the pubs or playing footy together.

That's how it was back then. Sort the shit out, and once it's sorted 50 per cent of the time everyone can then get along. You can sort things out with a fist fight. Someone wins and then you walk away. Nowadays it's the coward's way—pull a gun, pull a knife, do a drive-by. I've never carried a weapon. Not my style.

By the time I was 16, I was done with school. I was playing football for the school team, and in many ways I wanted to stay on and keep doing that. I was also helping out the younger kids with PE, and training the younger kids in football and I really liked it. But I was sick of school and the lessons. My parents didn't care either way what I did. I got my drivers licence (first time I might add!). Soon as I got my licence, my stepfather Ray gave me a job going the markets and picking up stock for his shops amd just driving to all of them and dropping it off.

Not long after I left school I bought my first car, a blue Escort GL. I was the first out of all my mates to get a car. It beat hanging outside shops or even walking from district to district, which Lee and myself did a lot just to get out of the area. Now we had a car, we could drive everywhere and look cool. We would blast out the music and roll our windows down to impress the girls. We would go on the longest drives just to be seen in the car. Getting girls was a lot easier now as well.

One day, I picked up Lee and we went for a drive. Everytime Lee was in my car he would always control the stereo. We never messed around while driving in the car, like doing burnouts or anything like that—we just tried to look cool in it. As Lee was playing around with the stereo, he accidentally jammed the cassette in the stereo so I tried to help him. We were coming up to a four-way intersection on Menlove Drive. I had the right of way, and any cars coming from the right- or left-hand side had to stop and give way to me. But as I approached the intersection a truck carrying diesel just didn't stop and went straight through. We went straight underneath it. We weren't even speeding. All I remember was looking up and seeing this truck in front of us and not being able to do anything about it and Lee shouting 'fuckin' shit'. Slamming on the brakes didn't help. We hit the truck bang in the middle of it and were dragged by the truck another 20 yards until it finally stopped.

The only thing that stopped us from going all the way under the truck was the truck's tool box. My car hit that as we went under. It also stopped us from getting killed as the bottom of the diesel tank stopped inches short of my windscreen and the bonnet of my car was crushed. When Lee and I got out we couldn't believe how bloody lucky we were. My car was a mess. We couldn't even believe we had walked away from that unharmed. We shouldn't have survived.

We both started laughing at each other. I think we were in shock still ,and we didn't know what just happened. We walked back to Nan and Grandad's after the crash, instead of getting a lift from the bizzies who turned up soon after the crash. And that was the end of my car and us driving around looking cool. We were back to walking.

I really wanted to be a football player, so I went round to all the teams doing trials. In those days, to get a scout from a team to watch you, either the team had to be good and always in the paper for winning or the player had to be good. Once you were invited down to a club for a trial, you only were given one game to show them what you could do. Now you are asked to turn up for a few weeks, and they put you through your paces, not just in one game. So I kept going to trial after trial, up and down the country, keeping up my fitness, doing boxing and going for runs.

Ray's businesses weren't going so well and he wanted to sell them off. This started a family feud with my mum's brother, Uncle Kevin, over a business deal Kevin and Ray had done. I was very close to my uncle Kevin at the time and I looked up to him— he was my favourite uncle. I would go and watch him play footy every Saturday as he also played for the Allerton and he was also close friends with my dad, even though my mum and my dad were not together anymore. Plus Kevin was good friends with John and Colin Smith. I didn't get into the dispute Kevin had with Ray, but I was dragged into it anyway and in the process, gained an enemy for an uncle. It was sad and to this day we don't talk.

The Muscle

When I went back to the UK to visit my dad in 1995, I went to visit my mum's mum, Nan, who was sick in the hospital. Kevin was there and he started a fight with me in the hospital corridor. To this day, I have not forgiven Kevin for what he did and for some of the things he has said. There have been so many times I have been back to the UK for a holiday that I wanted to meet up with him and knock his head off, but my dad and family members have told me to leave it. Time will tell.

Ray and my mum started to talk about moving again and then, out of the blue, Ray suggested Australia. His father lived there and he wanted to go and see him. His brother George was living there as well, and he'd been telling Ray it was a good place for a fresh start. So without even checking it out, or going there for a quick visit, they decided to move.

Mum called me into the kitchen and said 'Ray and me and the girls are moving to Australia. Do you want to come with us or stay with your dad?'

I was gobsmacked. They hadn't even been to Australia. I went round to Dad's place immediately and asked him what he thought. I thought he'd beg me to stay with him, but he didn't. He said he thought there might be better opportunities there. If I stayed in Liverpool I would end up just like all the other kids. There were no jobs except in the clubs he ran. Lots of the kids were getting into trouble with the cops stealing cars and breaking and entering. Lee was getting into a lot of shit as well. 'Hey you can always come back', Dad said. 'Treat it like a holiday. If you don't like it then you can come and live here. Give it a go. What have you got to lose?' So I agreed to give it a go. It didn't really hit me that I was leaving my home and going to live in another country that was miles away.

At the time I was leaving Nan was ill and I was worried about her. When I went around to see Nan and Grandad before I left, it was hard to say goodbye. Me and my nan sat down in the living room by ourselves talking about everything. She was pleased for me, but sad to see me going. She had only just got out of hospital and was still looking weak. Her health had improved but it was more because she was seeing me and putting on a good front for me so I wouldn't worry.

I told Grandad and Dad later that I would not have moved to Australia if I knew Nan's health was as bad as it was. The last day before I left

England, I spent with my nan. I took her in Dad's car for a drive around Liverpool to see places she hadn't seen for years or since she was a little girl. She had never seen my dad's nightclub so I took her there and around the city centre, as my Nan just stayed mostly in the local area. We had the best day and my nan enjoyed it so much we even stopped and grabbed an ice cream together. I hadn't given Nan a hug and a kiss for years, since I was a small kid, but I gave her the biggest hug and kiss goodbye and said I would be over soon to see her and I would write every week to her. I said my byes to my grandad too.

Within two weeks of my being in Australia, Nan passed away. Words can't describe how sad I was. Sometimes I think that if I had stayed she would have got better. I still think about Nan and miss her dearly even now. She was a big part of my life. She was more than just my nan, she had been like a mother to me.

So there we were in 1992, me, Mum, Ray and the two girls packing up the house at Huyton. Ray's mate Frank bought the house from us and even took my dog Duke off our hands. We didn't think it was fair to take the dog with us all that way. I left a lot of things I didn't think I would need over in Australia and I wish I had taken them now.

When the day came for us to leave, I spent the morning with Dad and he dropped me off back at the house. When I got out of his car he said to me, 'See you later Neil,' and drove off as if he was going to see me next week. I looked back at my dad and I could see him looking back at me. He had such loneliness in his eyes. It was so rare to see such emotion in his face—it's an image of him that has stayed with me forever. It's like he wanted to say more but didn't, but that's always been my dad. He has never been good with goodbyes.

PART TWO
Down Under

6

Where the Hell is Wollongong?

Ray's dad lived in a place called Wollongong. Ray's brother met us at the airport and drove the scenic drive along the coast through the national park. He was taking us on the scenic route, the Ocean Road, to try to impress us. But I looked out the window and saw this windswept coast and all I could see was masses of trees and one or two houses tucked in behind them. Oh my god! I am not going to last here! Where are the shops and the clubs? Shit, what I have I done moving over here? All I could think of was that the place reminded me of an Australian TV show set in the country, called *A Country Practice*. I thought we were moving to a city!

Coming from a big UK city like Liverpool and going to a small town on the south coast of New South Wales like Wollongong was a big shock. Wollongong's a relatively big city, with a steel industry, and it has colleges and schools. But it's nothing compared with Liverpool.

One great thing about Wollongong, though, was the beach. All the beaches along that part of the south coast of New South Wales are immaculate. They aren't like the big beaches in Sydney, like Bondi. There's hardly anyone there and the water is really clean and blue. I headed down to Towradgi Beach at the end of the road where I was living. It was quiet, had a good amount of white sand and medium-sized waves. Not too big for this scouser.

It wasn't a really hot day, the sun was out but it was really nice to just laze in the sun and go for swims into the sea. I went for a snooze, then I'd head out for a swim then lie back on the beach for a snooze. I woke up after a few hours and I was so stiff and sore and I couldn't move. I headed to the showers and looked at myself in the mirror. I was as red as a beetroot. I just couldn't move. It took me over an hour to walk home and the pain was so bad I wanted to cry. My eyes were watering and my skin was tight from the sunburn. I felt like someone had just picked me up and put me on a grill and cooked me. I had to stay out of the sun and at home for two weeks while my body and my face started blistering. That was a massive shock to the system. I always tanned when I went overseas but the sun here was a lot different to the likes of Spain.

Living in Wollongong, I felt like I had stepped onto the set of the Australian soapies, *Home and Away* or *Neighbours*, where people just walked into your house from the back door, letting themselves in. That wouldn't happen in Liverpool. If anyone walked into your house from the back door in Liverpool they were robbing you. Everything was really neat and clean. My mum liked it. You could tell this was our home now, she wasn't going back to the wet and cold weather of the UK. She was talking it up so much that she was trying to get my second cousins to live out here. I thought it was lonely and boring. I would call Lee and Tommy a lot back home, which didn't help. It just made me homesick even more.

I started to make a few friends playing football (or soccer as they called it in Australia). My first team was with the Wollongong Wolves and I also played for a team called Fernhill in the off-season. I was pretty homesick and missing everyone, but playing for the teams cheered me up. They really made me feel welcome and looked after me. I made some good mates who went out of their way to help me settle in. The soccer boys would take me out a lot, but only to local venues. The end of year trip away we went to the Gold Coast in Queensland, which has a whole street full of clubs. It was my first time up there, but all the clubs I wanted to go to that were like clubs back in the UK, the others didn't want to visit. They would all hang at a retro music club, which was playing all the 1970s and 1980s music. I just couldn't get into it. Listening to Midnight Oil and Jimmy Barnes just wasn't me. I felt like I was stepping back in time and yet I was only 19.

Waves in Wollongong was a nightclub all the boys liked to go to. The first time I turned up I saw a massive line-up outside the club to get in. I thought 'Wow this could be good'. Then I got inside and found the place had five pool tables and everyone was just standing around like they were at a pub. There was no atmosphere at all. The people weren't really dressed up either, they were very casual. Everyone was in surfy gear, like checked shirts and jeans. I felt really over-dressed in my dress pants and collared shirt. In Liverpool you wear your best outfit to go out. When I partied hard on the dance floor, doing different dance moves, everyone stood around and watched me as if I was some sort of act. Everyone else was just doing the side step. It wasn't like going out with Lee and my mates back home that's for sure.

There was one guy at the Waves club who kept taking the piss out of me for dancing and would start mouthing off at me when I got outside. I tried to keep my cool in front of my soccer mates, but they weren't doing anything about him. I wasn't going to be made a fool of, so I started shouting back at him to 'Come over here and see me.' The guy yelled back 'Get back to your own country you pommie fuck.' At that point I lost it and I walked over to the guy and knocked him out with a punch to the side of the face. As he was lying on the floor all his mates backed off even though I was shouting, them to come on and have a go. That night I knew that I would always have to fight any battles that came my way by myself. I didn't have Lee or any mates like I did back in Liverpool. I would have to earn a reputation not to be messed with. I never went looking for a fight with anyone, but no-one was going to fuck with this scouser. After that night, every time I went back to Waves a few people would come up to me and say 'Mate, great punch the other week.'

We were only in Wollongong for close to two years, and then Mum told me that she and Ray were moving again. Ray's business was in trouble and they were packing up. 'So it's up to you now Neil. You can get your own place here, or come with us, or go back to England.' I was 20 years old. I couldn't believe my mum was doing this to me again. It had taken me ages to settle here and now they wanted to up and move again. There was no chance that I was moving again, so I told her I was staying. I was so pissed off at my mum doing this to me that I stopped talking to her for a few years. It was like she didn't care about how it would effect me.

I was working at the markets and in a fruit shop in Wollongong. I was earning good money and I could pay rent and still live comfortably so I moved out and rented my own apartment. I was still really missing my mates—Lee, Tommy, Dad and Grandad so I rang them all at least twice a week. The holiday feeling was definitely wearing off. My dad would send out the local *Liverpool Echo* newspaper to me every week without fail, which made it worse in lots of ways. It kept me up to date with what was going on back home and I kept up with the football results, and what Lee and his brothers were doing in their boxing. There was a time when it was my birthday, and all the lads back home would pass a card around the pub and sign it for me and my dad sent it out to me. It was nice that they were still thinking of me, but it kind of made matters worse by making me homesick.

7

One Big Party

It took me about two years before I started to enjoy myself in Wollongong. I had a great boss who knew my situation and would always make sure I was OK, inviting me over to his family dinners and barbecues. I even became good friends with his son. They were a Greek family, who took me in as their own and helped me out a lot. I have a lot to thank them for, and they offered kindness and help when I needed it.

For my 21st birthday I organised a get-together at the Corrimal bowling club. I know it doesn't sound like an exciting venue for a 21st, but all I wanted around me was all my close soccer mates. It wasn't going to be a big deal, and lot of my friends then were much older than me. A few days before my birthday one of my mates rang me. 'Let's hang out at the beach for a bit.' We sat on the beach talking about soccer and what everyone was doing and who would come to my birthday. I thought I heard a scouser accent calling out my name. I thought I was hearing things or it was the sound of the waves on the beach. Then a *Liverpool Echo* newspaper was thrown on the ground where I was sitting. I looked around and there right behind me was my bloody dad! I couldn't believe it. I was in friggin' shock, lost for words for the first time in my life! It was the best feeling. I hadn't seen my dad in three years. He had come over the night before, found out where my soccer club was and got in touch with someone who told them who I usually hung out with. That's how he surprised me, the old bastard. That made my 21st at the bowling club all the better and Dad met all my mates.

Dad kept talking about his new nightclub, Club 051. He brought me over pictures, videos of the nights and tapes of all the DJs playing there. I already knew about it from my dad's letters he would send me, but it just made me more homesick and I really questioned what the hell I was doing all the way over in Australia when I could have been there working in that club. I already knew how good this club was from my mates. Everyone I knew went there of a weekend. One night my mate Stewy rang me all the way from UK just to see if I could get him into my dad's club!

Club 051 was the best nightclub my dad was involved with. He loved going to work every day. In the mid-1990s, it was probably the second largest nightclub in Liverpool and the only club bigger than the famous Cream nightclub. Club 051 had a really young crowd. People from all over the northwest of England would travel every weekend to come there. There isn't a scouser alive who hasn't stepped inside Club 051. That's why it was called the Scouse Club. The club itself was built underground and it went back underneath the road it was built on. You would walk in and pay at the front counter and then you would take the stairs to go down even more. When you got to the bottom of the stairs it would open up to a huge dance floor with a large bar and the DJ booth up high overlooking the dance floor. There were stairs that led to other chillout rooms that also overlooked the dance floor. The club could hold up to 2,000 clubbers. The crowd would be going off, high as ever and just dancing to the DJs until they were lathered in sweat. Even if you didn't want to dance, you would still go there because it had such a great atmosphere. The DJs that played there also made the venue what it is today, with Dave Graham and Lee Butler mixing the decks. Butler was known to have a line of coke on the decks while playing his set. Some line if he did that! The club also hosted big name DJs Roger Sanchez and David Morales

Every week, hundreds of people would be queueing up for an hour before the club opened. Hearing Dad talk about the club, made me realise I really wanted to work in the club industry. I wondered if I could be a DJ or maybe run the bar.

In the end, the local police pushed the council to close 051 down, and they won—it was too well known for drug dealing and there was a bit of gang violence there. It was closed in its prime, and there were certainly worse venues than 051.

I decided to come back to the UK for a holiday just after my 21st birthday. When I arrived, Dad met me at the airport and we drove back to Allerton. It was my first visit back, and I couldn't believe my nan would not be there. We went straight to see Grandad. I kept thinking Nan was going to shout out, 'What do you want to eat Neil' from the kitchen or the garden. Everything was still in the same place where Nan had left it over three years ago. My grandad was in a lot of pain. I could see how much he was still missing her. So we sat together and just talked about her to each other and by the end of it we were smiling again.

I stayed on for a bit in Liverpool, and signed up to play for APH, the team my dad played for on a Saturday. I actually got to play in the same team as my dad. This may sound a bit over the top but it was an honour to play alongside him in the same team. After all the years of watching him and seeing everything he won in the game was great for me. I had been to all the Allerton games since I was seven, and to play along side my dad was a cool moment in my life. There are not many people who can say they have played alongside their dad at a decent level at sport. I didn't know what to call him on the pitch—Dad or Geoff. Even the supporters on the sideline were joking about it. I remember the first time we played in the same team and just before the game started I said to him. 'What do I call you?' He said, call me anything, just not Dad, but I forgot and in the middle of the game I called out 'Dad, pass!' All the opposite team players started laughing and taking the piss out of my dad.

All my mates were doing the same thing, sitting in the same place in the same pub, waiting for the weekend to blow their money, and then having no money on a Monday all over again. And my mates who had been anti-drugs were now passing pills over to me. I couldn't believe it. Tommy was in the navy and Stewie was working for the council, digging on the roads. Lee worked with Stewy on the roads. It was a big shock to see mates who were anti-drugs now not even thinking that it was wrong to take them. When Lee passed a pill in my direction, I said no thanks. Lee said 'Come on, Neil, it's not every day I get to party with my best mate anymore, let's have a fuckin' big night'. Then he told me to just take half, so I did. Then later on I took another half and I did end up having one of the best nights out. From that night after taking half a pill started me on the road to party drugs in a big way. Every night after that while in Liverpool I would take one to two pills a night every time we went out partying. The feeling was like when a new beer comes on the market and everyone likes the taste of it. That was me with pills, or E's as they were.

I guess my dad is fairly typical of all the Cummins men, in that he never shows much emotion. When it was time for me to go back to Australia, he drove me to the airport, dumped me quickly and said 'See ya next time Neil.' He gets in a hot sweat and panics. If I haven't seen him for a while, he gives me a big hug, but when it's time for me to leave he can't cope. So I went back to my place in Wollongong. I could have worked for my dad if I wanted to come back, but whatever I've got, I've got myself. That's the way I like it.

After a while I started to get a nickname around Wollongong as the pommie boy or the big pommie boy or the scouser. I didn't go around looking for trouble but there was always someone who wanted to start some kind of fight with me to prove himself. Don't ask me why. Maybe it was my presence I don't know. I just always seem to stand out from the rest. I think it was more that I was English. I also made a lot of enemies from being a hard tackler playing soccer.

My attitude had changed since being picked on at Waves. I wasn't going to take shit from anyone. I didn't care who it was. I started boxing training again, but instead of hitting the bags I would do five of three-minute rounds with a brick wall like I used to. I loved hitting the wall and seeing the bricks move. I always thought if I can hit this brick wall that hard no-one would stand a chance if I hit them and it was true, most people I hit never got back up. I bought myself a weights kit and would train six nights a week. I was trying to put on size—and it was taking so long! Eating more food wasn't doing it for me. I started looking at videos on health and watching the WWF wrestling on TV. I started getting DVDs on bodybuilders like Don Yates.

If we weren't playing football on a Saturday then we would be out on a Friday and Saturday night, drinking until the sun came up and still I would be taking a few pills when I went out too. I wasn't too heavy on taking them, but I would always have a few on me in case. Plus a few of my soccer mates would take them too. In the late 1990s, the Wollongong club scene had a few good venues, but not many. Here's Cheers had a restaurant downstairs and a little nightclub upstairs, which generally had about 20 to 30 people there. It was dying and didn't have any atmosphere. I was friends with one of the security guards who also became a manager of the venue later. He said to me if I could help him get people down to the venue then he would look after me. So after every game on the weekend I would take all the soccer boys down there. Then everyone got to know about it and it became the place to be. I was always looked after and never paid for drinks and got my mates in for free. If I wanted someone kicked out who I didn't want in there then he was kicked out. I went behind the DJ booth and pretended to be a DJ for a bit. Here's Cheers became the number one place in Wollongong to go out to and it was great to see it grow. The Glasshouse was a good club too. Sometimes at the clubs I would spend 20 minutes just talking to the doorman or the manager, sussing out the venue and asking them how it was going. I was fascinated with the industry.

By the time I was 26 I was getting bored with Wollongong. It's a small town where everyone knows your business. I had really tried to push forward with my soccer career, but I was starting to pick up a lot of injuries from it. The season I had just had, I tore the tendons and ligaments in my knee and also fractured my ankle in the same tackle, which saw me out of action for five months.

From an early age I had wanted to be a soccer star and play for one of the big clubs. But I was realising it wasn't that easy, and without any encouragement from a club I was slowly losing interest. For the first time in my life, football didn't mean that much to me. At this point in my life I was going out more and drinking, partying and taking drugs.

I loved going up to Sydney and spent all my weekends there. A few of my mates had never been to a Sydney nightclub before, so I thought I would treat them to a place I'd been going to for a while. I took them to Hugo's in Kings Cross. It was the place to be seen back then and still is in many ways. It was very hard to get into. You had to dress up to even get a look in. It was a sleek and sophisticated cocktail bar and nightclub.

There were about seven of us. One of the guys had tried to get in a few weeks ago, but had been knocked back and was told he had to be a member. So I called up Hugo's and I asked for the manager. I introduced myself to him as Steve Highway, a coach at Liverpool Football Club. I had to give them a real name of someone there, just in case they did a name check. I told the manager of Hugo's that I had seven football players from the UK training and that they'd like to come to Hugo's for a relaxing night out. I told the manager that we had a training session on that night but wanted to come to Hugo's for dinner. I said that as we would be late getting there we would like a private VIP section away from everybody if possible, and I would be very grateful. The manager replied immediately saying 'I would love to have you guys come at our venue. Whatever you need on the night just let me know.' He gave me his personal mobile number and told me to call him on that the night we were coming. He said there will be no charge to get into the venue and that he would greet us on arriving and he would also give us two bottles of champagne and a drink tab.

I told the boys the night was all sorted. They were in heaven; they couldn't believe it. On the night of going there I called the manager and told him we were on our way. He had everything arranged for us when we got there. I told him that I would only be dropping the players off, but there would be a player who would be in charge of the group for the night called Dominic Matteo. That was me. Dominic played with me at Liverpool when I was there and he was the same age as me. He was just starting to make a name for himself, but wasn't too famous which was good. When we pulled up just outside Hugo's I told all the boys to remember that we were soccer players from the UK and when we were greeted at the door by the manager to act like one and shake his hand to make it look real. I must admit it was hard keeping a straight face.

We walked in like royalty. The manager and security told a bar staff member to wait on us if we needed drinks at the table. Everyone in the club was looking at us, wanting to know who we were. It was so funny to see. We had the best time and partied there all night. At the end I made sure no matter how drunk I was that I went up to him and thanked him. That night still goes down as one of the best nights I have had out with my soccer mates.

Over in Perth, where my mum and Ray were now living, my half-brother Jamie was born. Overnight, Ray and my mum became obsessed with Jamie, and Ray, who was never what I would call warm to me, noticeably became cooler. Gradually the calls became few and far between. They weren't interested in my life, and there was nothing much we could talk about. I couldn't believe my mum had dragged me 15,000 miles to Australia and left me. She didn't ring me for my birthdays or bother coming back to Wollongong even for my 21st birthday. I felt like I no longer had a mother. It was like she had her new family and I was a reminder of her past life that she didn't want to know about. I stopped calling her altogether as well, as I got the impression she was not bothered about how I was living my life.

8

On the Doors

I wasn't one for sitting down and playing the pokies in a leagues club or having a drink and waiting around to see who won a bloody meat raffle. I was in my 20s. It was time to party and party hard. My mates were like my family now—Jason and Nick, Azza and Hughsie, Steve the black stallion and little Greek George, whose nickname was Hagi after the Hungarian soccer player who was five foot tall. And Gaff my partner in crime when we went out—what a legend. We shared a house and looked out for each other. They were always there for me if I needed them. We partied nearly every weekend after playing soccer. Even sometimes going out the night before a game, but we never did that too much, but when we went out it was an all-nighter.

There was a fair amount of drink going down and the odd joint, which was a funny experience. I remember having my first joint at the house before we went out. Fuck, that was funny. After taking it I couldn't move from the chair, even though I was trying to get up. My body wasn't letting me move. All the boys were going to me 'Come Nelly let's go', but I couldn't move. I was telling them I couldn't get up but they were just cracking up.

Evenually it wore off and I could move my body. I experimented with acid too. Now that was freaky—just to see what it was like. I took it late on in the night while I was out. I had already taken E's in my life and I had learnt what a trip could do to me. It made me jump out of my bedroom window. I was lying in bed and the trip suddenly started working and I felt like the walls were coming down on me. I was freaking out and panicked, so all I remember doing is opening the window and jumping out. Bloody good job the place I was living at the time was only a single-storey, that's for sure. Things were different now. I wasn't that bothered with my soccer as I used to be, and drinking and taking party drugs was a common thing for me now.

I went back to the UK for another holiday to visit my dad. As well as being part-owner of 051 he had also the same arrangement with Garlands, which was a gay club. Even though it was a gay club a lot of straight people went there and while I was visiting there my mate Stewy wanted to go clubbing at Garlands. I loved it and the music and atmosphere was unbelievable.

The customers were roughly 50/50 straight and gay, and the crowd was trendy and upmarket. A lot of celebrities and footballers liked to go to Garlands because they knew they wouldn't get hassled by anyone. I even bumped into an old football mate there who had turned professional, Tony Warner. He was playing for Liverpool at the time as a goalkeeper. I had known him since my Liverpool youth days. It was the first gay club I had ever been in and Stewy was telling me to go the bar and by a bottle of rush.

'What the hell is that?'

'All the gay guys are into it. You will see it there at the bar. It will give us a buzz while we are here,' he said. So I went and got one and had my first bottle of rush there. It was a liquid that gave you a 15-second buzz, but it would also give you a massive headache if you took too much of it. You could buy it for about ten pounds behind the bar. Bloody good stuff. When I'm out with Stewy I always do something stupid and rush was one of them. Stewy loves to party and he went to the bar to get drinks and came back with two drinks and a bottle of rush. He goes 'Just have a sniff of that.' It nearly took my head off. I just remember seeing stars and dots in front of me, but the thing is you can't stop sniffing it once you've had it. That's why the first bottle was empty so quick. The next morning I had the biggest headache from it.

Lots of my mates took time off work to come out with me while I was home. We hung out at the Allerton pub or at the Heath pub. We got into a few fights in the pubs while I was back. I stayed with Dad in Aigburth and my Grandad's in Allerton for about eight weeks. Then I headed back down south for a few days to visit more family I hadn't seen in a while. I really enjoyed myself during this time back, but I think because I was more of a party animal this time around and I wasn't in shock seeing the drugs getting passed around in front of me by mates I thought didn't take them. On this holiday I took coke (cocaine) for the first time. I remember playing pool in a pub in Wavertree while on a night out with all the boys. We had already taken a couple of pills each and then all of a sudden a bag of coke got put on the pool table. About 5 or 6 lines got racked up and we had them before heading into town. It gave me that extra kick with everything else I had taken, but I do remember is I liked it and wanted more.

After that holiday to the UK, back in Sydney it was non-stop. All the soccer boys were now into pills and wanting to party just as much as I did. Even if I wasn't going out that weekend they would be pushing to come out. It was game on! All 15 of us went up to the Chevron Towers in Surfers Paradise for an end-of-year trip away and booked into a huge four bedroom apartment, which had a massive living space and balconies on the front. We were on the 16th floor. We didn't stop drinking and popping pills. One night, we even crushed some of the pills we had and started snorting them. That holiday was just drugs, drugs and more drugs. The amount of pills and coke that we had while up there, it's amazing we didn't fry our brains. One night we were on the balcony drinking, waiting for the clubs to open. I'd already had a few, let's put it that way. I was charging, having been drinking all afternoon and then taking two pills. I climbed over the balcony railing and started walking from one balcony to the other on the outside of the balcony, not even thinking what I was doing, knocking on the windows while some of the boys were in there rooms getting changed. The next morning I walked out on the balcony and looked down and couldn't believe what I had done the night before. I hate heights at the best of times and to think about what I did scared me. Drugs make you do stupid things, that's for sure.

I got a job doing security in Westfield Miranda in Sydney. The morning shift was pretty boring, going around the centre opening all the doors and car park entries. The rest of the day we watched cameras and walked around the centre. There were some perks when we would check on the cinemas to make sure kids were behaving and we would just stay there and watch movies.

We had a really good team at Westfield and the people who you work with always make such a difference to your job. They made it worthwhile for me. In those days if you were working in security you could chase someone for stealing, even if they ran all the way to Cronulla. Nowadays you can't even touch them. I must have over 100 stories about working there and what we would get up to from chasing thieves down the train tracks, to gang fights on a Thursday night in the food court.

Some of the benefits of working there was that you could go shopping whenever you wanted, eat whenever you wanted, and take breaks when you wanted. Plus it was a great perve. Car park patrol was the best in the summer time and nearly every guard would be up on the rooftop sunbaking and just waiting for a call if needed. I remember being up there one day and it was so hot that me and Frank, the other guard I was with, didn't want to move from sunbaking, so every time we got a call to do something we would say we were looking for a car for an old lady. We used to have the best tan by the end of the day.

David Jones was a great shop for robbers and we were always being asked to look after them. One day I was called to David Jones after two guys had stolen baby, men's and women's clothes. I knew it wouldn't be too hard to find them from the way they were described—from their clothing and what they looked like I could tell they were junkies. So I decided to go looking in the carpark, because from what I had been told they kept coming back to David Jones and taking more stuff. I thought they must have a car. I got to level 3 of the carpark when I saw two guys at the end of the carpark acting weird. As I got closer I knew it was them. I radioed for back up. The other guards were either busy or looking elsewhere for these two guys. So I quickly moved towards them cornering them by a car and the wall of the carpark. They still had one bag of clothing on them. I again radioed to other guards that I had them cornered in the carpark, but they were too far away to help. So I made a move. As I got hold of one, the other one ran at me shouting 'I'll fuck you up if you don't let my mate go.'

I shouted back, yeah try it. By this time I had the first one in an arm lock. Because I thought that the other one would run at me, I threw the first one to the floor against the wall, blocking him from going anywhere. I then turned my attention to the other one. I told him 'Come on then, come fuck me up.' At that point he reached inside his pocket. I thought he was going to pull some kind of knife or blade, but he pulled out two needles. One needle I could see was used, the other one had liquid in it. He started pointing them at me going for my face saying 'I'll stab you if you don't let my mate go.' A few times he came close to my face and all that was going through my mind was 'I am going to knock you out!' The next time he came at me I just remember smashing him with a right-hand punch, knocking him clean out and hitting him once more for doing what he did to me. I was pissed off having two needles put in my face. I really wanted to hurt them both more after he had tried to stab me with needles. But I was pulled away from them when the other guards turned up. I'm not even sure if the police charged them. When it all happened not once did it go through my mind about getting stabbed with the needles or even fearing the worst of what would happen to me if he did stab me. I just was angry that they had tried it on.

Night shift was about doing nothing but playing on the computer, reading magazines, eating and sleeping, which was an easy shift. One early morning a man committed suicide, jumping from the top floor all the way down to the cinema level. There was blood everywhere. I had only just started my shift when that happened. I started to look around for another job. I had my security licence and wanted to be more than just a security guard in a shopping mall: I wanted to start doing door work at nightclubs.

It didn't take me long to land my first nightclub gig. I remember going to the interview for the job and meeting two blokes called Shaun and Neal at the Rocks in Sydney. I was nervous as I hadn't been for a job interview before and I wasn't sure what questions they would ask or what they were looking for. I had never done door work before so didn't know what to expect.

They were looking for a doorman. When I got to the interview my palms were sweating and I was nervous about shaking their hands. I went to the toilet twice to wash and dry them. I was meeting them at a café and I remember sitting there and seeing two men walking towards me. One was quite big and the other one more slim. He looked a bit like James Bond. Within two minutes they had relaxed me and we were getting on fine. They were very easygoing and both were from the UK. Neal was Scottish and sometimes it was hard to understand him. Both had been commandos. Shaun was still one, but while he was back home he would run a lot of the nightclubs the security firm had. It took them 10 minutes to say I was just what they were looking for and and straight away I was put in the deep end. After only a week I was told I was head doorman. I couldn't believe it.

The place was called the Harbourview Hotel. It was a pub at the top end of the Rocks just under the Sydney Harbour Bridge. It was a nice little place. It had three levels, and on the top floor, an open balcony cocktail bar. It was open 7 days a week and I was there from Thursday to Sunday. I thought it was a great first place to start working on the doors. A few weeks went past and I had brought a mate to work with me there. He had worked at David Jones doing security at Westfield. It worked out well as we would travel to the pub together after work or car pool up from Wollongong where I was living at the time.

I started to get my own team together at the venue. It was up to me to decide who was good and who wasn't. I had a few dramas there with patrons, but nothing we couldn't handle. I enjoyed my time at the Harbourview. It was place where I could learn the trade, but after a while I wanted bigger and better venues, and a bit more of a challenge.

Being a good doorman is about controlling your fear. The best doormen will tell you they are scared and that's what keeps them alive. Whether you are dealing with the biggest villian in the world or a drunken 70-year-old man, you are always scared all the time you are at work. You are standing on a door for hours on end and you have got people hitting you, stabbing you, bottling you, spitting at you, threatening to shoot you or kill you.

No matter what, you always have someone in your face. This fear was the beginning of something that I took with me to every venue I worked at.

The pay rates are not that great and there are plenty more jobs that you can get a lot more money for. Depending on who you are and where you work, the rates can go up. During all the years I worked on the doors I came across a lot of doormen. Some did their job well, but a lot of them were all show. When I was working the door I would give the venue I was at 150 per cent of my attention every night. Some of the doormen I have seen working only give the venue 50 per cent. The rest was spent talking to girls or wanting to look cool. I was always picky with the doormen I worked with and if I didn't think they were up to it at that venue they wouldn't be back working there the next week. I wanted the doormen to be like me and give everything to the venue they were at—just like I did. I have always treated every venue I have worked at like my own. A lot of doorman these days just think that if you can pump yourself up with steroids you instantly become the best doorman ever.

I had my eye on another place that the same people owned, called Home nightclub, which was in Sydney's Darling Harbour. That was the venue at the time I wanted to work at and hopefully become head doorman. I knew they wanted me to work there, but I wanted to learn my trade first at the Harbourview. I started dropping hints that I wanted to work at Home. Then I got a phone call while I was at the Harbourview asking me if I could go to Home nightclub when Harbourview closes. I couldn't wait to finish so I could go there.

When I got there I saw Neal standing at the door. This was his venue. He had his own spot at the door where he stood. Just right of the main entrance on a ledge overlooking the crowd outside so he could see everyone in the line-up. Neal was cool to work for. You knew where you stood with him. He gave me a role at the venue and that is what I would do week in, week out. You could tell he had been in the armed forces by the way he stood and talked to you.

The venue was well thought out. It had three levels, each on a split level. It had six different rooms, including the balcony outside. There was staff for everything there at Home. We had two different door hosts, two people doing the tills, two people to do the stamps to get in, two first-aiders on hand, six bar managers and 25 doorman and many more staff. It was the most organised nightclub I had ever worked at!

I have a lot of fond memories of working there and I made lots of friends too. After a month or so Neal pulled me aside and said he wanted to give me a new role at the club. I was eager to hear what he had in mind. My current job was roaming the club and then, when every level of the club needed to close, I would close them. Sometimes I would go on the door for the last couple of hours. My new role was to find the dealers in the venue or anyone who was carrying drugs, be it male or female. My job was to watch people, follow them and check them and if found with anything I would escort them out to the front of the building were we had a 'garden'—just a few little plants by the main entrance. We called it the magic garden.

When I would catch someone I would bring them out to the front and make them stand by the magic garden. I would get them to turn and face the video camera so we had their face. Then I would get them to empty their pockets, wallet or bag depending on wherever I found it on them. When I did catch them with anything on them inside the club I would never take it from them. I would make them put it back where they got it from until we got to the magic garden. When they were outside, I would say to them to get out whatever I had caught them with and put it on the ledge on the side of the magic garden. So if they had say five pills of ecstasy they would put them on the ledge. I would have a guard who worked with me as a witness. The pills would be on the ledge and I would say to the person 'Are these pills yours?' They would say yes. Then from behind one of the little plants in the magic garden I would grab a little mallet. I would either use it myself to crush the pills or I would make the person who had them crush them. Sometimes I would have males crying after they or myself had crushed whatever they had. If they had coke I would make them sprinkle it on the magic garden and that's how I would say it to them. It's funny seeing grown men cry. I think I'm still on record for netting the most drugs caught there. I think it was close to 150 pills and one haul was four bags of coke all in a little empty box of mints. That time we didn't take him to the magic garden. We called the police.

The Muscle

At Home bar I had my first taste of the Sydney bikie culture, when suddenly the barstaff called upstairs and said the doormen had just let in a large group of Rebels bikies, all wearing their colours.

Now for those who are unaware of the bikie scene, the Rebels are the largest outlaw bikie gang in Sydney. The were founded by Alex Vella, who is the National President. The manager asked me to deal with it and see what the problem was. I didn't mind them coming in, but they can't be wearing their colours—it's too intimidating and you lose all your regular customers, I knew that much. I looked over to where they were sitting, watching them for a while to see who was in charge of the group. I picked out their group leader, the guy telling everyone where to sit. I called him over for a chat with me, one on one. I was nervous, jumpy, wondering if I had any backup behind me. I wasn't scared of confrontation but I never put anyone on show. I just pull them away from the public. That's what gets people's backs up. I explained to him that I had rules and that I didn't mind him coming in, as long as he didn't start shit and they take their colours off while in the venue. Then they can stay as long as they want. He told his boys to take their jackets off and they did. It's not all about being hard sometimes, doesn't matter who you are and who they are, it comes down to respect. On leaving the club they asked for me and shook my hand when they were leaving.

The security firm I was working for at Home nightclub did heaps of corporate events as well, and I started being asked to look after celebrities. One of my first ones was fashion model Mimi McPherson (Elle's sister) at a modelling show on Sussex Street in the city in the VIP tent. It was pretty cool what they had done for the event, basically making a laneway into a club. The organiser said 'Just make sure no-one goes near her if she doesn't want them.'

'How do I know who she wants and who she doesn't want?'

'You'll know. And if you don't you'll never make it in this job.'

So I just hung around and made sure no-one bothered her. British singer Craig David also came to Home nightclub—he had his own entourage of bodyguards, so I had to walk around with him and all of them as well. They would look after him, but I was to look after all of them. You never know when you're in a club if someone who is really drunk is going to try to take a swipe at someone like that. Or worse was girls coming up and trying to grope him and get a photo.

I didn't like working at Home nightclub when it was gay night. I just felt uncomfortable; it was just so over the top. I have no problem with gay people, but Gay Nation was too over the top even for me. All the gay guys were on the main dance floor. Most of them all had their shirts off and a few were dancing just in their undies. All security were told before the night started was that we could not touch anyone tonight if they got out of hand. The organisers of the night brought in half a dozen of their own security (who were also gay) to work alongside us and they would do all the man-handling if needed. We would just be back up. We were also told if we didn't want to work we didn't have to. I had the job of escorting a few of the acts and some of the DJs through the crowd on the main dance floor. I always got stopped and pinched on the arse and no I didn't like it, if you are thinking that! The second floor was for lesbians. They were all dancing away with their tops off and tits hanging out, all pashing each other. I know that might sound good for some people to watch but they weren't the hot lesbians you might be thinking of. They were all in leather.

Before Home nightclub became a straight club it was a gay club, which explains one big surprise the doormen and I did find working at Home nightclub—an unused door by the diabled toilets. This door led to a passageway that went behind the men's toilet. The men's toilet at Home nightclub has TVs on the wall while you do a piss and also while you are standing there doing a piss, the wall in front of you is a mirror with water flowing down it. We found a dozen or so chairs all placed neatly in the passageway, and couldn't work it out. Then the big surprise came when we figured out that the mirror on the wall where you piss is actually see through from the other side. So putting two and two together this was where you came to pick who you fancied. It was like a VIP area where you could see who had the biggest dick. Plain and simple that's how it was! I enjoyed lots of good times at Home nightclub, but then the team and management went different ways and when that happens it's not the same anymore.

Qantas at Sydney airport were looking for security so I got a job there, checking planes for weapons or the carpark for cars that shouldn't be there. Sometimes we'd find pilots and hosties who were too busy getting to know each other to get off the plane! On a hot day we would take our time and get a complimentary suntan. Fashion designer Peter Morrissey was designing the new uniform for Qantas and I was asked to model the pilot uniform. I had no problems with that but I was 120 kilos and I don't know any pilot who is that big. We couldn't get the jacket to fit me!

Working for Qantas meant cheap flights to UK when I wanted to and, even though the rates were good and the shifts were easy, I missed the club scene. Clubs are where I belong, I know how they operate, and I wanted to get back into it as soon as I could. I took a job at the big Irish pub, the Cock 'N' Bull in Bondi Junction, where the Guinness flowed seven days a week. The pub was full of mostly Irish backpackers travelling through Sydney. Sydney Swans players would sometimes come and have a few there as well.

The Cock 'N' Bull owner wanted me to clean up the crowd. He was getting a bit of trouble from the customers and when I started there were about three or four fights a night. The problem was that the pub was packed all the time, seven days a week. At closing time it was hard to get the fighters out. They just didn't want to leave. It was their home away from home. If you kicked them out they wanted to brawl. Every second person in there wanted a fight.

The owner told me I could have the final say on who came in, and he wanted me to look after the security there. This meant I was working as in-house security, directly for the owner. So on my first night I stood outside watching all three entrances to the pub, making sure the doormen we had hired let in the right crowd. But they were too weak and just let anyone in. I needed security guards who could handle themselves and work as a team and get to know who were the troublemakers to filter them out before they got in. It was going to take me some time to get this place under control.

My technique was simple, but fair. I would go over to the guy getting out of hand and without trying to put him on show in front of his mates quietly tell him its time for him to leave. If he just kept on drinking I would tell him again but firmer. Normally he would then start swearing at me so by the third time, I would drag his ass out of there—any way I could. I gave everyone three chances to listen and walk out themselves, otherwise

I had to use force. Then I'd have to take on their mates as well. I always came out the winner. That was how it was always handled back then. Now security guards have 20 cameras on them and they can't touch anyone, even if they get spat on or someone hits them. No-one understands the abuse doormen get from people when they have had a few drinks.

The cops also wanted the venue cleaned up. I think they were fed up with all the shit the Irish travellers and the locals used to start. Sometimes they'd bring in the sticks they used in Irish football and we would have to defend ourselves with chairs. Often the guys would want a fight and egg me on to start something.

The biggest brawl I've ever had to deal with is probably at the Cock 'N' Bull with Lincoln, my flatmate, who also worked there. We needed to kick out a group of guys but they didn't want to leave. You have to be so careful when you're walking people out of a pub like that because it is packed with people drinking and you can't move. We always needed at least four doormen to go in to remove someone, just so they could get the group out through the crowd. People had mates in the crowds, so as you walked out you would get sly punches. We had to watch each other's backs. We didn't back down but when we finally got them out on the street, they just wanted to go toe to toe with us.

After we had chucked this group of guys out, they started throwing objects at us from across the road. As soon as all the guards were out the front of the pub, we charged at them and cleaned them up. We cleaned them up good. If we did something like that now the cops would arrest us, not the guys making trouble. It's so weak now being a doorman. It's OK for someone to spit and punch and throw things, but you can't do anything back.

When they all ran off, we went back inside. The cops turned up and took a few statements, and then someone rang and told us that they had a tip off from the other Irish pub, the Tea Gardens, that the boys were coming back for round two. And this time there were about 20 of them. We didn't know whether to believe it or not, but just to be safe I called up a few extra guards to come down when they had finished their shifts. The cops kept coming past making sure everything was okay.

The Muscle

We decided to close the pub early that night, thinking there was going to be a riot. We only had five doorman on and I had messaged another three to come past in case. Just as we were shutting up the pub we saw a few guys hanging around across the road. Then more came. Then there must have been at least 20 guys waiting across the road. We still had bar staff in the pub, but we couldn't let them out in case something happened. All of a sudden, a heap of objects started to be thrown at the doors of the pub. I could see a few of them had empty bottles in their hands and one had a baton of some kind. The manager quickly locked all the doors and left one door open if we needed to surprise and charge at them.

When all the guards turned up, we all stood behind the door waiting. Then we opened the door and ran out. Until that point, we had no idea that there was so many of them, and that we were seriously outnumbered. They had bats in their hands and were throwing bottles at us like baseballs. We quickly ran back inside the pub and shut the doors. That sparked them off and they ran at the pub, trying to smash their way in. We put chairs and tables against the doors and they smashed the windows on the doors. They were like animals. They didn't care that this was their own local pub that they were smashing up. Luckily there were two sets of doors at the front of the pub which kept them at bay for while before they could get in. I could see out of the window that another one of the guards I called up for extra back up had just turned up. Brendan was sitting across the road in his car. Now Brendan was a mad bastard. He loved a fight, and would sometimes go around looking for one just for something to do. He got out of his car looking like something from the Matrix, with a long black leather jacket on. I called him on his phone and told him to drive around the back so we could let him in.

The cops had been called but they were taking forever to get there. We had to do something until they showed up. The Irish blokes were all busy trying to break down one of the doors that ran off the footpath. We decided to open the other door and run down to that door and surprise them. So we armed ourselves with pool cues and pool balls in socks and just ran at them with everything we had. A few of them ran off and the ones that stayed got a good flogging. Finally, the cops turned up half way through it all and couldn't believe what had happened. They said when they were tipped off they didn't believe it would happen. A lot of the Irish guys that started it were caught on video and the cops sent them back to Ireland. Looking back, I should have called for more boys to come down instead of sorting it with what we had there. I could have called the cops straight away, but I just wanted to teach those boys a lesson.

No matter what, after nearly every fight I had at that pub, the punters would come back the following week and say sorry for what they did. There was no come backs, it was just 'Sorry, can I go back in now.' That's how it should be. Not like other venues where if you give them a hiding they come back with their brothers or their cousins and second cousins with guns and drive-bys. It was sorted there and then and forgotten the next week.

There was an Irish guy who was quite a big bloke and he used to walk around thinking he was the man. Like he owned the place. One night he definitely wasn't the man. I told him he had to go and he didn't want to leave. He was doing his best to put me on show in front of everyone saying 'Ya renta cop, I'm goin nowhere.' I was always fair with people but if you start to make me look like a peanut in front of everyone then I'll knock your head off. I just grabbed him by the hair and threw him outside and then all of a sudden he takes his shirt off and starts saying 'Come on, come and take me on.' What is it with people when they fight and they take their shirt off? Do they think it gives them extra powers or something? It always happens with me when I kick someone out of a club. They always want to fight me with their shirt off. They must think it turns them into a transformer or something. So there is this bloke with his shirt off dancing around like he's Muhammad Ali. I just walked over and dropped him with one punch and he was on the floor. Game over.

At the Cock 'N' Bull I was in charge of all the doormen and if there were any fuck-ups it was me who copped it. I was obviously doing all the right things, because in 2002 the managers asked me to run another venue they had in Kings Cross called Soho/Yu. This was big—a job on the doors in Kings Cross. Bring it on! Most doormen work for a security firm that has the contract, but at Soho/Yu I was working for the owner. All the guards there liked me being around and didn't mind the thought of me running the door, even though the security firm they worked for didn't like it.

The Cross has been the place for drinking and partying for a long time, with sailors coming in from the naval base at Garden Island and heading for the red light district which is right in the middle. Crime, police corruption, drug dealing, prostitution, gambling, both illegal and legal—it's all there. It's got the country's first legal medically supervised injecting centre to help junkies try to kick the habit and the place is right in the middle of all the nightclubs. There are big hotels there and small ones, pubs, clubs and restaurants. It's the kind of place that only comes alive after 10pm at night for tourists, locals and everyone in between. Kings Cross has got some big landmarks—the massive Coca Cola sign on the corner of William Street, Darlinghurst Road and Victoria Street is the most famous. And it's had big names operating there, from Tilly Divine the famous brothel owner to nightclub owner Abe Saffron, who was called the 'boss of the Cross'. I knew enough about the Cross to know that's where the pumping clubs were.

My first job at Soho/Yu was to look after the cash register and stamp the punters. The guards who were doing it before me were letting a lot of people go in without paying and the club was losing money on the door. I got to meet a lot of people that way. Then the management asked me to be on the door to choose the kind of people who would come in. They wanted me there to pick a sexy crowd and not let just anyone in. That was a big job and a lot of responsibility. I'd never done it before and for the first weekend I was pretty nervous. I had to be quick on the decision but because I had been on the stamps I got to know the crowd. I decided to pick people as if it was my own club. 'If this was my club who would I want in?' I wanted people who didn't cause any shit, who came and enjoyed themselves, dressed nice, had fun and spent money.

Yu was for young 18–25-year-olds, funky-looking city types. My strategy worked—it was one of the busiest clubs in the Kings Cross. Word got out it was a clean crowd and a good environment so all the young ones came in. I learned to look down the line and see who was coming up next. You don't have time to stop people and chat before you let them in—it's got to be a fast decision on a busy night. If you dithered, some of the guys would have a go and start arguing and fighting with you. You had to make all your noe's clean and quick and move on. At Yu there wasn't that much trouble. You would get the odd person who wanted to be a hero but he was brought straight back down to earth with my right hand. Mostly they would all leave with no hassles.

Upstairs, Soho was a different crowd and a club for people over 25. Jason the licensee was a top bloke. Straight away we connected and worked together well as a team. I knew what he wanted for the club and he knew how I worked. I called in the best doormen I had known from the Cock 'N' Bull to come with me. When I was working, none of the doormen drank or popped pills. We were there to do the job and handle any incident if it arose. You had to be sober for that.

Brendan was on the doors there. He would do anything for me and loved working on the doors. But he also loved to fight, which let him down sometimes. He would always have my back and that's what you need when you're doing the doors. To this day, we are still good friends.

Brendan's only problem was he was easily led and loved to party. Sometimes he partied too much. He later joined the Rebels bikies.

A lot of celebrities came to Soho/Yu. When the Miss Universe crown came to Australia in 2004 on the head of Jennifer Hawkins, all of Sydney wanted to be her friend. One night I was told to come in early to work because Jennifer was coming to our venue. She turned up and came into the club with a few of her friends. I had to follow her around for four hours to make sure nothing happened to her. It did my head in. Her entourage were a bit snotty and thought they were better than everyone. She kept asking my doormen to get her drinks. Who did she think they were, her butlers? I would tell them not to.

When I first started in security my goal was to run a door and then to become a bodyguard. I modelled myself on Steve Segal, the martial arts expert and action film star. He had real presence and I really liked his style. Not that club work was always cool. Sometimes you were just cleaning up the mess of some people's lives. Once an Australian celebrity couple came in with a British celebrity couple and, after it got late, one of the guards called me to check out the toilets and see what they were doing, they kept going down there in twos. I thought they are doing coke for sure but when I got there we could see through the gap in the toilets the Aussie woman getting fucked by the British guy. I couldn't believe it. We kind of made it known that they had been seen but walked away. I went back on the door and then I get another call to come inside and down to the toilets. I thought surely not again. This time it was the Australian guy fucking the partner of the bloke we'd seen before. When they were back in the booth I walked slowly up to them and told them that it's best that you all leave and go and get a room to have your swingers party at.

When I worked at Yu there was a taxi driver picking up females in the Kings Cross area who he'd then try to sexually assault. We were told to watch out for any taxi's that didn't look real. You know I always tried to better myself. So if I heard something like that I would be looking out for it even while picking the crowd on the door. When I heard about this taxi driver he'd already assaulted two women. At the end of the day that could be your partner or sister getting into that taxi. Every weekend I was looking for him and I also made sure that any females getting a cab was walked to the cab by a doorman, who would take the cab numbers licence down and rego. I also warned a lot of females to not to get a cab by themselves. They got him in the end but that was scary time trying to find the fucker, as we'd been told he had picked up a woman from Soho.

While I was working at Yu word got around about me in the Cross. People started saying something along the lines that the doorman down at Yu is a big cunt or he knows how to fight. 'Don't mess with Neil' was the rumour as he doesn't take shit from nobody. I didn't care who you were and that went for every venue I've worked at. This was my venue now, my rules if you want to come in. This is what I wanted since getting my security licence to be head doorman to a big nightclub in Sydney. People had to know that if you fucked up in my venue that you had me to answer to and I wouldn't take your shit no matter who you were.

While I was working at Soho/Yu I did a few shifts at the Eastern Hotel in Bondi Junction. It was owned by the same owners as Cock 'N' Bull and Soho/Yu. I didn't enjoy it as much as the other venues I had worked at.

The venue had only just opened and wasn't as busy as it would be in later years. The venue was connected to Bondi Westfield. It was a big venue. Three floors, but it wasn't busy when I was there. It was mostly the same crowd as the Cock 'N' Bull when I was working there. I think that's why I hated it—I didn't want to work at a venue like that again. The only good thing was Lincoln was there working with me. They wanted me to teach the guards what I had done at their other venues, but it wasn't happening for me there. It was more of a pub at the time and I was over pubs. Think I was there for about four months, then I left and told them to put my mate Lincoln in charge.

While working at Yu I started dating one of the barmaids, but that didn't last long as I found it too hard to date someone I worked with. A few months later I started seeing this girl who would come down the club every Saturday night. She worked at Myers in the city. She was a lot younger than me. I dated her for a few months but I wasn't really ready for a relationship. Soho/Yu was a place were the girls would throw themselves at you. They wanted to know you as you were their way of getting in and getting in for free sometimes. Believe me back then some hot girls went to that venue.

One night at Yu in the early hours of the morning a guy turned up at the door. He'd obviously already had a lot to drink. I was on the door.

'Mate, it's a bit late mate and by the looks of it, you've a bit too much, not tonight mate.'

'Do you know who I am?' he asked.

'No, I don't,' I said 'Why don't you enlighten me?'

'I'm Dave Auld, the licensee and manager of Dragonfly up the laneway. Who do you think you are?'

'I'm the head doorman of Soho and Yu of Victoria Street,' I said back.

He started laughing.

'What's so funny?' I said.

'At the end of the day you're just a doorman doing your job. In the meantime, I'm the licensee of Dragonfly and do you know who owns that?' Dave asked me.

'Not really and I'm not interested,' I said.

'Well you should know who owns it because he can make you lose your job just like that,' he said and clicked his fingers.

'Well mate,' I said, 'I don't care and you're still not getting into my venue. You are a licensee of a venue and yet you are turning up to get into another venue the way you are. Would you let someone like you into your club?'

'Well if they are as good looking as me I would!' he said and he made me laugh. But I still didn't let him in. A few weeks later he came back sober and apologised for his behaviour. After that we became friends, and he would invite me up to Dragonfly for after hours drinks. That's how Dave Auld found out about me when he met me for the first time. Don't get me wrong, now I know Dave he is a top bloke and I have a lot of time for Dave, but when he drinks he is a nightmare.

Another time, I had to deal with someone known in the Cross as Sunny. He was a stocky Islander., who would always try to get in, if he wasn't pissed or trying to start fights with someone. I had already had a few words to him over the way he acted, sometimes telling him to leave. But this particular weekend I was told by Jason, the licensee, that Sunny was no longer welcome as he had tried to get behind the bar the previous weekend to get to the till and had also threatened the barmaids, even grabbing one of them by the face.

I knew he would come past as he always did and right on queue, he arrived and tried to get in. I pulled him up and asked him what he thought he was fuckin' playing at by doing what he did. He started yelling at me, asking me what I was going to do about it. I got ready to line him up with my right hand if he did try anything. I could see him clinching his fists and tensing up. At that point he yelled, 'Come on then, bro'. I didn't hesitate— I landed a right punch to his face and dropped him. Brendan, my fellow doorman, ran over to help but Sunny was out cold, with a bent nose to go with it. We picked him up and put him in a taxi and told the cab driver to take him out of the Cross.

I knew doormen who would take coke, pills or shots on the door. If I found out they never worked for me again—if you are not on the ball there's no point being there. A lot of doormen came to have a perve, or a laugh, and didn't care because it was just a second job. That's the attitude

I didn't want. I was working all the time and training, and didn't have time to drink. But when I went out I wasn't afraid to party. If I did go out and party and, even if I was off my face or had too much, I would always make sure I didn't make a fool of myself at the venues I worked at or other venues that knew me. That's why I know I got a better reputation because of that.

Dragonfly was the latest incarnation of a club at that address. It started out as Tunnel nightclub, which was a well-known place for the underbelly of Sydney to hang out in the 1980s when the cops were running most of the drug supply in the Cross. Then it became the NRL player magnet that was Dragonfly. Dave had told me off for not knowing someone who was nicknamed the 'King of Kings Cross', John Ibrahim.

9

Bikies and Strip Clubs

It's not surprising that I got to know a lot of bikies over the years, working where I have worked and for who I've worked. I've become friends with a lot of people from all different bikie gangs and made some enemies too, although not by choice. I never want to make an enermy but that's what can happen in this industry because of your associations with the people you've worked for. Over the years I've had a lot of confrontations with bikies at the venues I've worked at. There are a few who respect your decision but then a lot of them think you're putting them on show. At the end of the day, I'm just doing my job. If someone from another club went into their clubhouse, surely that person would have enough sense to just turn around and leave—that's the fuckin' same as my venues. That person would be mad to start a fight, and that's how they should be when they're told they can't come into a venue. Just walk away and try somewhere else—fuck, it's not rocket science.

At Soho/Yu I met a whole cross section of people that were different to the Cock 'N' Bull crowd. There were celebrities for a start, who would want to be seen in the right places. And then there was the 'underbelly' crowd, people going under the radar and mixing it up, but still wanting to be seen in the clubs.

One of the doormen had a friend called Hooksy. He was really polite, although he looked like a bulldog. He had a bald head, stocky body and gold chains around his neck. He didn't smile much, just had a look on his face that said, don't fuck with me. I first met him when he came over and shook my hand. He said he was the national president of the Bandidos outlaw motorcycle club. He said if I or any of the doormen ever needed him, to just give him a call. None of the bikies would go to their club with their colours on. If I knew some guys from a bikie group were inside, then I would stop anyone from another club going in. In the months ahead, we became very good friends. He was a gentleman, a really nice person, respectable. A few years later, he was gunned down in Crown Street.

Mick Howie, the national president of the Comancheros Outlaw motorcycle club, came down to Soho/Yu one night after being released from jail. Mick was always a gentleman. He was a stocky, well-built guy with short dark hair and a goatie. He was with a few guys I already knew and he respected everything I said to him about behaving in the club and taking off his colours. He just partied with his mates and left, shaking my hand as he did. He always shook my hand on arriving and leaving. He never started any fights at the venue and he would spend a stack of money there.

I ended up hanging out with Mick and his mates a lot and we partied hard. I hit the drugs big-time and I think I ended up taking everything under the sun—speed, pills and coke. I once even cooked the coke and smoked it. Drugs were like chocolate to me. I would take four to five pills every time we went out.

At Yu, I was kicking out a lot of dealers, and learning who they were. I'm not sure if that made me good at my job or not, as one of the main dealers I caught was a promoter at the club. I had watched him for months as he had that look that he was always up to something else rather than promoting. He used to do his deals by putting all his pills into cigarettes. Clever idea, if you think about it. He would sit on the pokie machines and one by one all these people would come see him and ask him for a cigarette. So one night I set him up and got a mate to ask him if he knew anyone who could get him pills. He said, 'I might be able to help you', and told him to meet him in the pokie room in 20 minutes. My mate sat next to him while he was playing the pokies. The promoter handed my mate a cigarette and inside were five pills. At last I had him, but when I went to confront him, he only had two cigarettes left with three pills in each of them. I told him he wasn't welcome at the club anymore and barred him. I was just glad I finally got him.

Not long after, I decided to take a break from the Cross and left Soho/Yu. Jason, the manager, left the venue and it wasn't the same once that happened. I took a rest for a bit to see what my options were. Lucky for me my reputation as a doorman was that I was tough but fair, and easy to work with. I got an offer to work at two gentlemen's clubs in the city, the Men's Gallery and Pure Platinum. Actually it was very boring! Don't get me wrong, you get to watch strippers all night, but there is no atmosphere there. And after you have seen a stripper's routine once, you've seen them all. It wasn't for me. I need to be on the go and busy, and working the mind not the eyes if you know what I mean.

At this time, I was living at Rockdale with one of the guys from the Comancheros. There were always parties going on. One night I came home from work completely knackered, so I just went straight to bed. An hour later, one of the boys came bursting into my room, jumping on the bed, pointing a gun at me saying 'Wake up Neil and party you boring fuck or I'm going to shoot ya.' I freaked out, because I could see he was off his head. I just kept saying stop pointing the gun, stop pointing the gun and tried to calm him down. Eventually he went back to the party, but it really freaked me out. I finally woke up to myself and moved to Bondi.

Two things would have happened to me if I had stayed there. I would either have been dead by now, or I would have joined the Comancheros. That's how close I was with them. I was also close with Daux who, at the time, was second in charge of the Comancheros and I was also good friends with fugitive Hakan Ayik back when I lived in Rockdale. He used to train at the same gym as me and we would hang around with the same mates at the time.

Another person I got to know was Richie Rich—what a guy. He is a gentleman and one of the nicest people I have ever met. I met Richie in

2002 while working at Soho/Yu. I remember the night he rocked up to the club. He came with about five or six guys. Not the type of person I would let into the venue. As they arrived at the door, Richie asked to speak to the head doorman, which was me. He spoke like a gentleman to me. Not like the usual wannabe gangster that I always got working on the door. He said, 'I just want to come in here with my friends, spend money and have a good time. If any of my friends play up, come and get me and I will deal with them.' My reply was 'If any of your friends play up, I will kick them out and you too.'

As I said, I always give people one chance, if I feel they should have it and with Richie Rich I did. There was something about him that made me give him that chance. That night was the beginning of a good friendship. To this day he has never let me down or disrespected me in anyway. I must admit, after a few weeks he started to bring in more and more of his friends to the club—people that I would usually not let in to a venue. But the reason I did let them in was Richie Rich never let me down when he came to the club. He partied and so did his friends. They never started any trouble and they spent lots and lots of money behind the bar and on the pokies (he usually won big on the pokies).

I became such good friends with him and his boys that I even started going out for drinks with him. They were party animals from Wednesday through to Sunday and if any shit went down—and it sometimes did—they could fight.

I remember the first time I went out in Manly, for one of the boy's birthdays. There were about 15 of us. What a night—we drank and we drank. I was smashed before the night had even started. Plus I had had a few lines of coke too. We were having the best time drinking, dancing—I was dancing on chairs and tables—and just being boys. Jason, who was the licensee of Soho/Yu, was out with us too. He had put money down on the pool table to play pool. He saw that the game was finishing and he was next on. I was standing about 20 yards away at the bar and just glanced up to look over and saw Jason arguing with two males. Then, about two seconds later, Jason was punched in the face. As soon as I saw that I ran over, shouting at the boys, 'Someone's just fuckin' hit Jason.' I ran over and knocked out the guy who hit Jason, then I knocked out his mate. The guys who hit Jason had four other mates by the table who joined in the fight. The fight was so intense that while I was punching one of the guys, I was getting hit on my back repeatedly with a pool cue. I was so pumped I didn't feel it at all. At the end of the fight, there was just guys all over the floor trying to pick themselves up. The doorman did nothing but, then again, what could they have done. He would have ended up on the floor with them. It was like a scene from a movie. Then we just calmly walked out the club.

Another time, at Hugo's in Kings Cross for my 30th birthday, I invited 30 of my closest friends.

I got people in there who would never get in. Richie Rich was running late and he was the only person from my guestlist who had not turned up yet. If you know Richie Rich, he is always dressed well. When he got to the door to come in he was told he wasn't allowed to come in, which surprised me. After everyone else they had let in and then to say no to him was fucked. He called me to tell me they wouldn't let him in so he was just going to go somewhere else as he didn't want to make any dramas on the door because it was my birthday.

I said, 'No way, it's my birthday and you're on the guestlist.' I went up to the door and asked the doorman what the problem was and he told me that I had too many people in there for my party. I said 'Are you serious, one more person is going to really change things.' By this time, there were about six or seven of us at the front door of Hugo's, arguing. The door host was a bitch, just saying no he's not coming in. The head doorman, Ray, was just being stuborn and didn't want to listen. As I walked away, saying to Ray you're fucked for fucking up my night. Afterwards, I heard a gun was pulled by someone. Or more shown, from what I was told. The next day I got a phone call from Ray saying he didn't mean to fuck my night up. I told him it was all good and he told me that someone had shown a gun because he wouldn't let Richie in.

Then about two hours later, I got a call from John Ibrahim, asking me what had happened at Hugo's and was everything okay. I was very surprised with that call and that he even knew me or my number, as I had never met the bloke. I actually became good friends with Ray after that night. I never did bring that up with John while working for him!

John Ibrahim is the second of four brothers known as the 'Ibrahim brothers'. The eldest son is Hassan (who I know as Sam), followed by John, Fadi and the youngest son is Michael. At age 16, John Ibrahim witnessed a family member being attacked. He got involved and ended up in a coma for threee weeks. He took six months to recover and now has a large scar on his torso as a result of that stabbing. When he was 18, John opened his first nightclub in Kings Cross, called the Tunnel, and slowly started building an empire to become King of the Cross.

Richie Rich later went to prison for six years for the robbery of $60,000 from Soho/Yu, which happened months after I had left. Even while in prison, he still sent messages to me through people saying hi and hoping I was well. I bumped into Richie Rich in 2009 while out at the Eastern in Bondi. He is still the same person. Top bloke.

Bikies have been around in Sydney forever. I never thought they caused too much trouble in the clubs if you let them know the rules. When I was working as a doorman for Soho/Yu, the bikies in Sydney were coming on the scene more in the media. They were running drugs, tattoo parlours, video stores and car washes.

One night, about 30 bikies from the Nomads motorcycle club rolled up. They looked like something out of a movie; the noise they made was deafening. They rolled up and blocked off the whole street so no-one could get passed while they parked in between all the parked cars. That was the first time I met Sam Ibrahim, who was the Parramatta chapter leader of Nomads. It's funny how you meet people in a situation like this and then you get to know them later on and just relax and have a few drinks.

This night they had come down to Soho in force. They had come down to show us who was bos after the other doormen and I had a run-in with a couple of doormen, who had links to the Nomads, who worked at another venue in the Cross. We had kicked them out the weekend before and then they wanted to fight us, which we were happy to do, but they shit themselves when we went to start on them and said they would be back.

When they came back they brought back up, if you know what I mean.

I remember all the Nomads getting off their bikes and walking over to our door. I was wondering what the fuck is going on. They asked to speak to the head doorman—me. I find it funny now, but when that question was asked every one of my doormen pointed towards me. Bloody shit-bags! I remember Sam getting in my face and asking me if I had kicked out two doormen last weekend. I said 'I kick out a lot of people.'

'You being smart, cunt.'

'No.' When he told me who he was talking about, I tried to tell him why they were kicked out, but really it didn't matter. Sam was Sam. He didn't want to listen to my story or why it had happened. He had come down to put it on me and tell me to let those doormen back. I never did and the Nomads never came back.

H was a member of Nomads and was, at one stage, a bodyguard to Sam Ibrahim. He was close to the family and we became very good friends. H was a legend. He was this big bloke with tattoos all over him, and then he wants to talk about soccer with me on the door. That used to crack me up and he fuckin' knew his soccer. From what I heard, he joined the Hell's Angels but that shouldn't have mattered. At the end of the day, H and I go way back and I have a lot of respect for him as a person.

I got to know a lot of Rebels over the years and became really good friends with a few. Some mates even joined them and, at one stage, I was asked to join back in 2006 but said no. I became really good friends with Ricki, who was the president of the Liverpool chapter of the Rebels. Top bloke. Respected me from day one when I first met him up at the Cross. His chapter was always welcome at our venues. They never fucked up and Ricki made sure of that.

If I ever did say to Ricki he couldn't come in he always understood why and never argued. He said if any of my boys fuck up kick them out and call me and I will sort them out. I would always try to get the president's number of any chapter that came down to the venues who were allowed in. The Nomads were the troublemakers. They could be dickheads, as the full members had too much to lose if they fucked up.

Brendan, a doorman I worked with, and I would go to the gym a lot together and he told me he knew all the boys from the Rebels bikies.

'Do you think I should join?' he would ask.

'You should stay out of it, and be your own boss.' I said. 'Don't work for anyone else except yourself. That way you stay in control. Why do you want to be told what you have to do and where you have to be all the time, and why do you want to join for?'

'It's not like that, Neil,' Brendan said.

'Not now, but wait until you join, things will change.'

He joined anyway, and soon after that he ended up in jail. I couldn't go to visit him—it killed me that he did that with his life. He should have stayed out on his own. Months before he joined the Rebels he asked me to get him into the Notorious bikie club, but I wouldn't do it.

Another bikie I became good friends with was Wayne Sneider. We became friends when he was with the Finks and we stayed friends after that. I would always look after Wayne. I remember I was at North Sydney Police Station over an assault I was on and in popped Wayne to sign in. I was there talking to the Gang Squad taskforce, known as Raptor Squad, and Wayne walks behind me and grabs me and says, 'Big fella, where've you been.' I'll let him into any venue I work at cause I know he won't cause any shit. I think he's with the Hell's Angels now.

I might not see certain guys from different bikie gangs for months or even a year or so, but when we meet up it's like it was only yesterday. I don't look at Wayne as a Hell's Angel. To me, he's just Wayne. It doesn't matter if the boys I know and work with are rivals, I will still talk to my mates from the other clubs. We just don't bring up shit about what's going on.

One night Hooksy and almost the whole western chapter of the Bandidos motorcycle club turned up at Pure Platinum. The licensee of the venue panicked when he saw them all, but once I told I knew them and they would be okay he calmed down. Hooksy shook my hand as he came in. I could see the manager and the staff members absolutely shitting themselves having 20 or 30 bikies in the club. I pulled Hooksy aside and asked him what was going on. He said it was one of their members' birthdays. So I told the manager to open the VIP room upstairs which is only used on weekends and give them a few strippers. He did that and they all went there. Hooksy gave me his word that they'd all behave and that was good enough for me.

Halfway through the night the manager got a call on the radio that the cops had turned up downstairs to do their usual walk through. I told Hooksy that the cops were doing a walk through, and asked him if his boys were clean. Hooksy said some of the boys were tooled up and asked if we had a back door. The problem with that was that it would set the alarm off. Hooksy started to panic, and then told all the boys to put their tools in a bin in the kitchen and one of the waiters would put it with all the rest of the rubbish. The cops came up and checked a few of the boys, then they started to leave. When I finished my shift, one of the boys came back and collected the bin. To this day, I have no idea what was in it.

I started to cut back on my hours at the strip clubs and got an offer to work at a new club that was opening on Oxford Street called Milk Lounge. It was owned by Todd O'Connor, but also had links to John Ibrahim, who I kept hearing about, but was yet to meet. The venue wasn't big, but I liked it and jumped at the chance to get back into mainstream clubbing. Todd gave me an opportunity to bring in my own DJs and promote nights on my own. I used to stay back until two or three in the morning doing guestlists and sending out invites. It got me into the promotion side of things. It was a good, relaxed atmosphere working there and we had a good security team on the door.

Todd had a reputation for being difficult to work for. He'd go off his nut if there were not enough people in the club or the promoters weren't doing their job. He liked to be noticed did Todd. He would park his car in a No Standing spot and if he got booked he would rip up the fine in front of the parking ranger. We were always joking about his weight and who was bigger, him or me?

About this time, in 2005, I met Tiffani Wood. She was in the girlband Bardot, created by a reality TV show called *Popstars*, with Belinda Chapple, Sophie Monk, Katie Underwood and Sally Polihronas. They were a success for a while. Now she had gone single in the music scene and wanted to launch her own new single at the club. When she came to Milk Lounge I was told by the promoter to walk her up to the lounge and make sure she was looked after with drinks and stuff. A few hours later she invited me up into the bar for a drink. I didn't know who she was when she turned up. Never seen her before. So when she invited me up for drinks I didn't have a clue what she was talking about and who the band was she used to be with. I kind of just nodded my head like I did know. But we hit it off and after that we started dating.

One day, John Ibrahim walked into Milk Lounge. Straight away Todd stood up. 'How are you doing John?' John was with about four people, walking in behind him. He looked casual, a baseball cap in the back pocket in his jeans. Casually dressed. I actually thought he would have been taller. You could feel his presence in the room. That presence made him taller than he was. I was working with the DJ and looked up to see this smooth-looking guy, who also had a really friendly face. 'Who's he?' I asked the DJ.

'That's John.'

'What? John Ibrahim?' I replied. That was the first time I had really seen him from a distance. You could sense the respect rippling through the place as he walked by.

Milk didn't last long—somehow the club ran down and the money it made wasn't put back into keeping it up. It was a pity as it was a good-looking club. Not long after that Todd went to run Goodbar club but was sadly gunned down and killed in a back street in Tempe, in the south of Sydney. That was a massive shock to everyone when that happened. I couldn't believe it when I was told. It was hard to believe. I just kept saying to myself it never happened, he will walk past in a minute and turn up for work. Then it hits you that it did happen. My memory of Todd is a happy one. Of a person who kept himself fit, loved the gym and loved his kids, but with an attitude that he didn't care about hurting anyone's feelings. He would walk around Oxford Street with a tight shirt on, pumped like he had just done a chest workout.

The funeral was huge, with nearly every code of bikies there and everyone you could think of from the underworld. One person missing from attending the funeral was Fadi Ibrahim. He was overseas at the time and I remember thinking how disappointed and upset Fadi would be that he would miss the funeral. Fadi and Todd were close. I remember sending

Fadi a message on my phone saying the funeral went well. I know Todd would be doing God's head in now, trying to open a nightclub up there.

I was asked to do some shifts at Goodbar on Oxford Street on Wednesday nights. It was owned by a guy called Eric, who was involved with John Ibrahim. A doorman who worked there was leaving and he had put my name forward to look after it. Goodbar had a sexy crowd with R&B music and a really mixed crowd inside. When you walked in, you saw a long hallway running down the building and then you could go downstairs to a dance floor or stay on the street level on a smaller dance floor. Like all the clubs it had a VIP lounge at the back. Every club has a VIP lounge to make people feel special. Back then if you knew the promoter you could get yourself into the VIP lounge. Goodbar had dark décor and it pumped.

Sam Ibrahim and I hadn't exactly hit it off on our first meeting. But as we got to know each other, we got on really well. If he said hello to you when he was coming down to DCM's you knew he was in a good mood. Otherwise say nothing. I remember John Ibrahim would say to me make sure that if Sam comes to the club with his boys they can't come in. When John would make me do this, I was the only person who would tell Sam he can't come in. John did this to me at DCM's a couple times and at Trademark and Dragonfly, and all the time Sam wanted to kill me, or his boys, who are supposed to be his mates, wanted to kill me too. I hated it when I had to do that. The last time it happened, John called me while I was at Trademark and told me not to let Sam in if he tries to get into Trademark. When I used to tell people what I was about to do if Sam came, they would fuckin' freak out and when he turned up they would all leave me. It was funny but a nightmare. When he turned up at Trademark he shook my hand asked how I was. I asked him to step away from everyone and told him I couldn't let him in until John arrived. I couldn't even finish the sentence and he went off. Saying, 'Who the fuck do you think you are, you and my fuckin' brother. Wait and see now what I fuckin' do to you, Neil.' Because I worked at his venues, John was my boss and whatever John said I would do. I only listen to John, no-one else. If John told me to do a certain thing this way I would do it the way he wanted it done.

The Nomads bikie gang folded while Sam was serving time. The members all went their separate ways while Sam got locked up. There's no loyalty in the world. One day you have a tattoo of a certain bikie club you're with and then a year later you're with a different one. That can't happen surely. How could you ever trust that person when he was with someone else with their name tattooed on him?

From that gang, the Notorious motorcycle gang was formed. I had a lot of friends in Notorious. You could say I was one of them, but I wasn't actually a member. I was their eyes in the Cross and at other venues and places. I was only close with them because of my friendship with my good mate, Samoan Dave. president of Notorious was Allan Sarkis, and Samoan Dave was Sergeant at Arms. When Dave got on it, watch out. He's crazy, that's why his other nickname is Crazy Dave. Dave's presence is scary. One of the scariest people I have met. He could take five or 10 people on and knock them all out. He was someone you didn't want to mess with.

Dave and me had been good friends for at least eight years. We had a very good friendship. I would meet up with Dave at least once, maybe twice, a week to have a chat about things and if anything needed fixing in the Cross or anywhere else. Dave trusted me with his life and I did the same back. If I ever needed Dave, he was only a phone call away. I was the only person who could answer Dave back and get away with it, and tell him it was time to call it a night if he was too pissed. I loved going out drinking with Dave. Just before my wedding to Mariana, Dave got put away for about a year and I was devastated as he was going to be in my groom's party, as a thank you for all the years of being there when needed. I've seen Dave in action when he has had a few fights and I'd say it would be a good idea to just fall on the floor before he hits you. Better off that way. Dave is a mate for life.

Later on, after I'd finished up at Goodbar and was back working in the Cross, for John Ibrahim, I was asked to look after one of his cousins, who was in the Nomad bikie outlaw gang. That night would change a lot of friendships between me and the boys I used to hang around with in Rockdale—Kanza, Ali, Mick Howie and all that crew. It all changed in just one night out at the Cross. I was looking after one of John's cousins, Ahmuddie, from the Nomads at the time. He'd not long got out of jail and I was told to stay with him while he went around the Cross. We started the night off at Porky's and DreamGirls. Then he decided to go to Sapphire Lounge. As we got to the front of the club, we bumped into the Comanchero bikies and a few of the boys from Rockdale who were going into the club as well. Straight away there was nearly a brawl between us. The Comancheros were going off at Ahmuddie and he wasn't backing down either. I was trying to calm down the boys I knew but they were having none of it and they were calling me a dog. I couldn't believe it, these were guys I had been friends with for four or more years. I had lived with one of them and partied with the rest. They just turned on me like that. Okay, so it was probably to do with Ahmuddie being there and me being with him because he was from a rival bikie gang. But to say what they did to me was low.

Ali, who was once a close friend, told me he was going to kill me. I slowly got Ahmuddie away from there and told him don't worry about them and let's just enjoy a night out. I took him to Yu club, where I used to work. We got down there and the doormen and the manager greeted me. They weren't going to let Ahmuddie in because he was all tattooed up, but because he was with me they trusted me. We were having the best time in there when in walked the Comancheros and all the Rockdale boys again! I couldn't believe it. We were standing by the bar as you walk in and they just walked straight into us. All hell broke loose. Thank god no-one had a piece on them at the time. Otherwise I think we all would have shot each other. We were totally outnumbered by them. There was about 10 of them and only three of us. Bottles were getting thrown and fingers were getting pointed. The doormen didn't know what to do. They were just trying to hold everyone back. Then one of the Rockdale boys hit Ahmuddie with a cheap shot on the top of the head and it was on even worse then. They kept saying they were coming back to shoot us and we were saying, come on then. I'd fuckin' had enough by now and one of them spat at us. As he did I reached over the doorman who was in between both groups and grabbed his shirt to drag him towards us, but they were finally pushed out the back door of Yu and were yelling at us that they were coming back with pieces.

Everyone in the club was screaming and wanting to leave. After five minutes they opened the front doors and let us out. Ahmuddie was all fired up but I calmed him down. He wanted to wait for them to come back, but I told him they wouldn't come back. I reminded him he'd just got out of jail and that there will be another day to sort it out but not tonight. I put him in a cab and got him out of the Cross. The Comancheros didn't come back that night.

While I was at Goodbar I met a person who changed my life—Nick Nadar. He was a great guy with the kindest heart. He used to be a bodybuilder. He wasn't too big, but he had a muscular body. He told me he looked after John and Sam Ibrahim and venues up and down Oxford Street. He was also a standover man at the clubs if we needed him. He was a true professional in that job, a regular bloke who just navigated his way through people and the clubs. He always sorted out fights and problems and hassles and he did it in such a cool way. I had a special bond with Nick. He would help anyone out who he knew.

Nick has fits every now and again while he's working. Sometimes I would have to make sure he was okay, as he would just collapse in front of me while he was on the doors. Even with that health issue, he would still do a good job. He was going through a bad patch in his life and he had problems. We all did—everyone has issues in their life that they are dealing with. We would talk on the doors about life and then for months. He never said anything to me about the fact that he would get really depressed, even though I was with him a lot. Then one day he killed himself at his unit. It shocked me, as we had become so close. I was shocked that he didn't tell me his problems. Hopefully you are at peace now, mate.

Some nights when we were on the doors we would get a call that John was coming down to the club to check out what was happening. We had to make sure that the club had the right people in there, and that the place was packed and busy. It was nerve-racking sometimes, as John would tell you straight up if he didn't like the crowd. I made sure all the doormen were working properly and weren't eating or drinking by the time John turned up. You always had to be on your toes when John came. Then he would go either to another venue of his or home and everyone would relax.

One night I was called in to Goodbar to work on a private function for some extra cash. When I turned up for work I asked who the function was for and no-one seem to know. Then a limo pulled up outside the door and out got Mick Howie and a few other Comancheros. I recognised one of the boys I used to hang out with, and asked him what was going on. He said they had booked the venue and all the boys were coming down. That's just great, I thought, the Comancheros have booked Goodbar and nobody knows about it! I was the only guard on duty that night because everyone thought it was just some little party for someone.

I messaged John immediately. He couldn't believe it. He said he would send down some boys to help me on the door. I called a security firm to ask them for more guards. This was a big fuck up. I was told to close the venue as soon as more guards came to help out. At that time, the Comancheros were Sam Ibrahim's rivals, and yet they had booked the venue. The club was shut down immediately. When everyone turned up the club was closed down.

So many people got into shit about that. Then on another night, the Comancheros stormed Goodbar. I was working up at the Cross and I got a message to come down ASAP as there had been gunshots at Goodbar. They had stormed the place, hitting anyone in their sights. I quickly got down there but by the time I arrived the cops were there and I wasn't allowed near the place. My mate Adam had been on the door when it happened. He told me that they just ran in and fired a gun a few times, punched the chick on the cash register and hit a few patrons and left. If I had not been busy working at the Cross that night, I would have been there. The rivalry between the bikie gangs was getting heavier. They were putting pressure on. After that, there were a lot of other shootings.

A few of Sam's boys would do any cleaning up that had to be done. They were standover men or they wouldsometimes look after Sam. They were associated but never became full members. One was Paulie. He would come hang around with John and Sam but mostly Sam. He was one of Sam's boys. He would do a bit of debt collecting or go around looking after some of the venues. I liked Paulie, he would always look out for me and was always himself—never tried to be somebody he wasn't. He was always respectable when out and if any of his boys fucked up when they were out he was first to pull them back into line or tell them they had to leave. He would always tell them that if I said they couldn't come in then that was it and to respect that. He was a top bloke.

Then you had blokes like Ahmad Glebe. What a wacko, but also a funny cunt when he wanted to be. One minute he would be talking to you normal and then he would just lose it. He was even worse when he was drinking. Good luck trying to get him out of a nightclub when he is pissed. Doesn't matter if you're his mate and you're just trying to look out for the bloke, he will turn on you. But he also has his good side too. He has been there for me in the past, but we have had our run-ins. His biggest problem was he didn't like being told no, like, 'No Ahmad, you can't come into the club tonight.'

There was another guy called Wack—real name Mustafa Assoum. He was a legend. This guy looked out for me all the time when I first met him. When he partied he was also hard to control. But when all these boys were off their heads on nights out at the Cross or at DCM's. I was the only person who could tell them, 'It's time to call it a night' and they would go. They might argue a little bit but they knew that if I said it was time I meant it and they'd better leave so they didn't give me the shits in case John found out they mucked up at the venue.

Wack passed away a few years ago now. He was gunned down in the street. Sad in a way as only two or three nights before he was shot he came past the Cross and came into Porky's for a bit. We were chatting about his kids and my daughter. He was all happy telling me about fatherhood and he was out of all the bullshit and enjoying life. He hadn't been hanging around any dickheads anymore and it was good to hear. I was shocked when I heard he was gunned down.

10

Is this it?

After about a year and a half of dating, Tiffani and I got married. Tiffani was heavily pregnant and so we had a quiet wedding in Byron Bay, which was published in OK! magazine in lots of glossy picture spreads. Dave Freeman, the son of underworld figure George Freeman, was my best man. John Ibrahim actually turned up at the wedding which was amazing because back then John was under the radar. He wasn't in the public eye like he is now.

Tiffani and I soon moved into a unit in Randwick and our daughter Lillian was born soon after. Lillian was a beautiful baby, just like her dad! I would spend a lot of time with Lillian during the day. She was a cute little baby and she is all Daddy. That's what I like.

While at Milk Lounge, Dave Freeman had pushed me for months and months to come and work at DCM's on Oxford Street. He was the head promoter there. I'd been there once on a night out with Richie Rich and I'd heard a lot of bad rumours about it. A lot of my doormen at Soho were with the same security company at DCM's, and they told me it was a lot of pressure and even at the cloak room you had to be on the ball the whole time as heaps of big names would come in all the time. My mate Brendan had worked there and he used to tell me he hated it as he just stood by the cloak room every night and not move from there. I knew it was a big club, and it had a big name and a high profile. I told everyone I didn't want to work there, because of the rumours. I actually thought it sounded like it was downmarket, a sweat box. But Adam talked me into it. 'Just do one shift and see if you like it,' he said. 'You can always back out. What have you got to lose?' Sounds familiar doesn't it? So I took on the job.

I can tell you on my first night I was as nervous as hell. This was really unusual for me, as most first nights I was fine. John was also involved in the club and I knew he was somebody with presence. I knew I had to perform well to get along there. Their plan for me was the same as all the clubs I worked at—clean up the crowd and weed out the people they didn't want coming in and get a funky vibe happening.

Only problem was, there were only two doormen, me and Pat. There were two lines at the door—the line of people coming in off the street, and the people who had booked and got priority, the VIP line. Pat put me on the VIP line.

'Listen up, Neil,' Pat said. 'No-one fucks up here if we let them in. Otherwise, see those stairs? They will be coming down them head first.' I don't think he was joking, but he did say it with a grin. I guess that was my induction course!

This was where I first got my nickname, the muscle. It was because of how big I am, especially the size of my biceps. Plus no-one would mess with me and everyone knew I would take no shit. When I later became John's number one security guy for all of his clubs, the media picked up on the name and it stuck.

After a couple of months, Pat took a back seat and I took over from him, picking the crowd and checking the ID cards. We also had a guy called Big Fadi, who used to be Sam Ibrahim's bodyguard, outside with us in case we needed him. Big Fadi was a big bloke—bodybuilder in his spare time and a school teacher during the week. Now that was weird, I thought. Big Fadi had a soft-spoken voice, but piss him off and he had a hard hit on him. I've seen the hits first hand. The biggest thing about Fadi was that he didn't speak much if he didn't know you. If patrons came over to him to get into the club he would walk away from them or just not talk, but once you got to know him he was a top bloke. There were more of John's boys upstairs. One thing I learnt from Big Fadi was that you don't punch people if you can help it. He told me punching someone leaves marks on the other person and you should open hand them. I tried it once and the guy didn't get back up. After that I never punched anyone again. That's a fact, believe it or not.

The atmosphere at DCM's was wild and unbelievable. The line-ups to get in were massive—people would start lining up two hours before we opened just so they'd be sure to get in. It was the only venue in Sydney playing high-energy dance music then and it could fit in about 1,300 people. It was a huge rave. It had a house room with a lounge and a high energy room. There were podiums everywhere and mirrors, and three major bars. They only hired the top DJs. Then everyone would collapse in the red chill-out room. This place pumped. I've worked at some good nightclubs, but even today there is no venue in Sydney that can touch DCM's in its hey-day.

One night, dead on midnight, a four-wheel drive came down the hill and stopped right in front of the club. All the four doors of the car snapped opened at the same time. Who the fuck is this? I wondered. Then out gets John, cool as a cucumber in dark blue jeans with a fitted collared shirt, sleeves rolled up and not a hair out of place. He was followed by the massive Tongan Sam, his bodyguard, who was wearing his trademark long black leather coat with a mullet, and then his driver.

I was trying not to look and stare wide-mouthed. I'm standing there all nervous and I can feel my palms getting all sweaty. John walks up to me and shakes my hand.

'Is that all you've got?' he says. 'What?' I stammer back.

'When I turn up, you grab my hand and shake it,' he joked.

'Fuck,' I said and laughed.

He winked at me and patted me on my back.

'You enjoying it here?'

'Yeah, it's good.'

He walked in and went up the stairs. Tongan Sam stopped too and shook my hand.

'How you going?' he said in his trademark deep voice and walked past.

I knew from that moment I wanted Tongan Sam's job. They were the coolest people in the Cross.

'I want that job,' I said to Pat. He just laughed.

'I do. I want that job.'

'Get back to work,' said Pat.

Dave Freeman and John wanted DCM's to be the best club on the street. They wanted me to be really strict about the people I would let into the club. So again I made my mind up to run it like my own club. Dave told me what he wanted from me and I just said to leave it with me Skinny. That was Freeman's nickname I had given him. So no more Nike or Adidas runners, no more sports wear. This was not Parramatta Westfield, I would tell people who turned up dressed like that. Also out were bikie tattoos, mullets and guys with rat's tails. If I didn't like your haircut you weren't getting in. If I didn't like the look of you, you weren't getting in. If I didn't like the shoes you were wearing, you weren't getting in. My rules. If you don't like my rules step out of the line and go somewhere else. Gold chains were another thing I hated. I was picky. And no big gold rings either. Everyone knew that if I walked along the line and lifted the barrier rope at the side of the queue where you were standing, you weren't getting in. You could see the nervousness on people's faces when I did my walk along the line, thinking I was coming to get them.

Some people would come back week after week and get turned away. Then finally they would beg me, 'What do I have to do to get in?' I would tell them but it still didn't mean I would let them in. Then you had the ones with the attitude when they were told to get out the line. They would try to be a hard dickhead in front of everyone, but they would soon come back down to earth when I left the door to approach them. A lot of them ran or they would say, 'I'm only joking'.

I wasn't scared to say no to people at the door. It didn't matter who you were, if you were in the underworld, bikie or in a gang. Even if there were five or 10 guys I had to tell to get out of the line I did it. That's what John liked about me. On busy nights, John would sometimes stand on the door a little longer to show his presence and to overlook the door. That's when you had to make sure the door was done right. There was a night when John was sitting on a stool at the front door and we had a massive line. I had a few mates in the line who were really borderline to get in. Only because of the way they looked, but because I knew them I would let them in. I shook their hands and said to them to go through. As I did, John overrided me and told them they weren't going in. They didn't say a word and they left. John called me over and asked me why I had let them in. I told him I knew them and that they were harmless, but it didn't matter: he told me he didn't want that kind of clientele in the club. Didn't matter if I knew them or not. After that I was even more careful about who I let in.

What was also cool was that a lot of the people who came were 18 and it would be the first club they went to, then by the time it closed its doors they would be 25. They basically grew up there, going there every weekend. DCM's was their life for six years. They became family in a way. I still get stopped now by people saying 'Oh my god, it's Neil! You let me into DCM's when I was only 18 years old.' Then there were other people who would stop me and say, 'Neil, you never let me into DCM's. Why?'.

When I took over the door everyone knew it was my door. I would turn up late every Saturday night just to let them think I wasn't coming to work and they would be thinking they would all be getting into the club tonight. But I would come from the back of the line and go down it telling people to step out of the line for whatever reason before I'd even started and opened the doors. Put it this way, if no-one saw me on the door by a certain time they would be making phone calls to their mates to come down because I wasn't there.

I was the only doorman that I know of who carried a pair of scissors to cut people's hair so they could get into DCM's. There was a lot of guys desperate to come into DCM's and they would do anything to get in. I wasn't always serious on the door and sometimes we would have some fun and a laugh to make the night go quicker. There would always be a guy who had the longest rat's tail down the back of his head and he would be pushing me to let him in and I would be telling him it's not happening.

New Year's Eve party at my unit—Bozza is third from the right, Ahmed Elrich is next to me and I'm on the far right.

Tangi and me on the door at DCM's. Behind us is the window that was hit by six bullets in the drive-by shooting.

Ahmed Elrich and me at the Melbourne Cup races.

The car of mine that got six bullets put through it.

Tarak Elrich, me and Ahmed Elrich at the Ivy Pool.

Adam, me and Ahmed—doormen from Wollongong.

*Me with John Ibrahim at the
Swiss Grand Hotel, Bondi Beach.*

Bodyguarding Fadi Ibrahim at the races, while talking to Dave Freeman.

The boys and I on a night out at the Ivy.

Mariana and me out at dinner for my birthday.

Salvatore Coco, who played Sam Ibrahim in Underbelly, *and me at my wedding.*

John Ibrahim, third from right, and me with the boys from the Cross at my wedding.

Me telling Tito to stop taking photos at the Tunnel nightclub.

Looking like the mafia, but running an hour late, on my wedding day to Mariana.

The crew outside DCM's—(back row) Tongan Sam (first on left), me, Tongan Sam's son Nim to my left, then John Ibrahim, Dave Freeman and Samoan Dave. Levi is pictured in the front, bottom right.

Right: John Ibrahim, smiling for once, at my wedding.

Below: Richie, Fadi Ibrahim, Shaydu and Peter Everett at my wedding to Mariana.

My son Cruz.

My daughter Lillian and me.

With John Ibrahim at my engagement party at the Bank nightclub.

Me, Alla and Ash at the Swiss Grand Hotel, Bondi.

Looking after John at Sydney Airport—Carmen Electra was checking in at the same time.

At the gym at my heaviest—130 kilograms.

My wife Mariana and I at the Piano Room.

Weekend away at the Gold Coast with the boys—Lynn, Ali, Me and Fono.

Then I would say, 'Well, if you let me cut your rat's tail off, I will let you in.' Even Freeman looked at me and was shocked when I said that the first time. The guy said okay you can! So I got the scissors and I cut his ratty off, which was a good 5 inches. That guy had grown that ratty for three years and had it cut off for a night out in DCM's. There were so many guys that did that. I had a collection of rat's tails just inside the front door where I kept the scissors.

I remember this funny moment one night, around 3am. The place was still pumping, but around this time you start to get fewer people. So you can be more selective about whom you let in at this time. Now this fit-looking guy turned up, but he had tattoos all down his arm. I thought he looked okay to go in, but before I said yes I thought I would play a game with him first. I made him wait outside in the line with just him standing there to see how much he wanted to come in. He kept asking, is it busy? When can I go in? At this point, I asked him how much did he want to get in? He said all his mates were inside. So I made a deal with him. I told him, 'I will let you in for free if you get down in the middle of the footpath and give me 25 push-ups.' He said 'No chance.' I said fine and told him to get out the line. He said, 'You're serious, aren't you?'

'Yes. Give me 25 and I will walk you in for free.'

He turned to me and said with a grin, 'This is fucked, I have never heard of doing something like this to get into a club.' I said 'This is DCM's mate, we're different to everyone else, now give me 25.' He got down and gave me 30 and said does that get me a free drink for the extra five push-ups? I said you wish and let him in. When I used to go upstairs to do a check-up or get some water to take down to the guys outside, I would always get stopped by guys wanting to thank me or chat to me while they were all sweaty saying thanks for letting them in. I hated that.

All the people in the club would sit in the same sections so you always knew where to go. The Maroubra boys would be by the pool table. The steroid boys would be on the podium or just underneath the DJ box. The girls dancing, who would wear next to nothing and wouldn't stop dancing all night, would always be on the podium. They were like the Eveready bunny advertisements.

One night, about a dozen Bandidos came down to DCM's. I told one of them to ring up John and if John said it was okay, they could go in.

'He knows I'm coming down.'

'Well, tell him to message me,' I said.

'Are you going to put me on show in front of the boys?'

'I can't even let any of our own bikie boys (the Bandidos) in, let alone you.'

He kept going off that I was putting him on show and that John knew about him and his boys coming to the club, but I knew John would never okay them to come in. I didn't care what he kept saying to me, they weren't getting in.

Then out of the corner of my eye I could see one of them reaching down his pants. He pulled a gun half out to make sure I saw it. One of the boys said, give it to me I'll do it. Then someone else shouted to put it away.

He shouted back to them, 'No, fuck him.'

'What, you going to shoot me, hey?' I yelled.

Then all his mates told him to put it away as he was attracting too much attention.

As soon as they left, I messaged John and he said he knew nothing about it. He was pissed off with them for pulling a gun on the door. I also messaged Samoan Dave. He rang me straight away and said he would come down if I needed him, but I told him it was all good, they had gone. When he finally turned up he asked who it was and how many of them were there. He got it sorted out privately.

Samoan Dave was always around, looking after the family. He was in the Notorious bikie gang and most of the Notorious was made up of Islanders and Lebanese. I remember Dave being pissed one night when we were out and asking me when I was going to join. Straight away I said no way, mate, it's not for me. I was an associate not a member. I must admit, I've never seen a scarier person than Dave. For a big Islander boy he was quick on his feet and had a very hard hit. He was always there if shit went down or someone tried to put it on in any of the clubs. Just before he got locked up, in 2010, we were going to start training together. We were going to do a bit of cage fighting and boxing to help me get fit as I was going to start boxing again and maybe have a few pro fights. I was disappointed because I was looking forward to training with him and was hoping to have my first fight in the ring with Dave in my corner. Dave had long dreadlocks at the back of his hair and he loved them. He thought he was sexy when he had them on and you could see it in his walk. People used to stop me and ask who would win in a fight between me and Dave. I said it would never happen. They would push me and so I suggested that the only way I would win is by taking him by surprise and pulling his dreadlocks off. Then we would probably have a laugh and stop fighting. I would tell them that we were brothers from a different mother. That's how close we were.

By now, the cops knew me as an associate of the Ibrahim family and were watching my every move. They knew I was very close to the family and could be getting used as a heavy, a standover man. Apart from John being around the clubs and having a drink with Fadi Ibrahim, I wasn't exactly doing any business at the Cross, far from it. My life was pretty straight—I went to work, I got paid, I partied and went home.

The cops tried to stop me from working and get me off the doors because they thought I was working for the Nomads bikie gang back in the DCM days. They believed I was the eyes and ears for them and that I was letting dealers into the venue. That's how well the cops do their job and get information—I was doing the opposite. I was keeping the dealers out. They might have been right about me being the eyes and ears for the Nomads but that was only to let them know who was around.

Then the cops thought I joined the Notorious bikie gang. So did everyone, really, as I was very close to all the boys. They still didn't believe me and for most of 2010 they kept stopping me and pulling me over while I was driving my car.

'Aren't you a member of Notorious?' they would ask me every time.

I would keep telling them that I wasn't. Then they would say I was seen hanging with them, drinking with them. I would say, 'Is that a crime?'

'Yes, I have mates who are with those gangs but I am far from being one.' What they thought I was doing I have no idea. They were trying to get me for anything. They finally got me for an expired security licence and told me I couldn't work anywhere until my licence was fixed up. I thought they were going to get me off the doors for good by telling the security industry to not renew my licence, but they didn't. So while my licence was getting fixed up I went to work at a smaller club called Lady Lux for a while as a door host. I was just doing pretty much the same thing, picking the crowd and not letting in anyone that shouldn't be going in. I remember even back in 2008 getting pulled aside in Westfield Bondi Junction by two coppers while carrying my daughter Lillian. They passed me and looked twice, then stopped and asked if I was Neil Cummins. I was carrying a man-bag at the time and they asked if I had a gun on me. I smirked and said no. They asked if they could check my man-bag. I knew I didn't have to show them but I had nothing to hide. So I opened it up to show them my daughter's bottle. It was doing my head in as everyone was walking past looking at what was going on.

After I got my licence renewed, I went straight back to work at DCM's. When I got back to DCM's, the crowd they were letting in was so bad it took me four weeks to clean it up. So I started all over again on the lines, pulling people out who weren't up to scratch. The other doormen had really let it go downhill.

Freeman was glad I was back. He told me that none of the other doormen would say no to the type of guys I said no to.

'They don't have balls like you, Skinny,' he would say to me. He had started saying Skinny back at me as a nickname because he knew it would piss me off. I was always trying to put on more size and weight.

At that time the tension between the Nomads and the Comancheros in Sydney was massive. Once I got a call from a private number and the caller said he was Daux from the Comancheros. He said he was letting me know that some of the boys were going to DCM's for the night and asked if that 'was going to be a problem for me'.

'You know I can't let you in.'

'What's the problem?' Daux replied.

'You know if you want to get in you need to ask someone higher up than me.'

He yelled down the phone at me. 'You're the man aren't you, or are you his bitch?'

'Can't help yah,' I replied.

'Wait till I see you. I'm back in Sydney next week, I'm coming to see you,' he said and hung up the phone.

They didn't turn up, but we did kick out of the club two associates of the Comancheros. The following week, Daux and some of the Comancheros boys came down and I wouldn't let them in. As one of them left he said, 'Watch your back, cunt.'

There were a few more tit for tat incidents with both bikie gangs after that. There were a lot of stand-offs between them and our boys, the nomads. Then one night I was down the shops at Randwick with Lillian. It was around 8pm and I was walking back to the carpark to get my car. Lillian was in a sling as she was only a few months old. As I was walking down the ramp to the carpark, I noticed two guys walking a lot more quickly towards me. When I got closer to the bottom of the ramp they had caught up to me and they yelled out, 'Hey, Neil.' So I turned to look at them. They were two Comancheros. I got to the carpark and they grabbed my shoulder and one of them said to me 'Where you going you hard cunt.' I said 'What do you mean?'

'We hear you and Big Fadi have been looking for us, well here we are, cunt.'

I said 'It's not the time or place, mate.'

'Let's go, cunt,' he replied.

'What, you're going to hit me while I'm carrying a baby?' I asked.

'Where's the baby?' So I showed him what he had thought was a gym bag. When they saw it was a baby, they both backed off and the other Comanchero said, 'Sorry, didn't know it was baby.' He then told me to tell Big Fadi that they weren't hard to find if Fadi was looking for them. And they walked off. As I walked to the car, I checked on Lillian to make sure she was okay and she was still asleep.

One night, not long after, I was standing on the doors at the club when a car full of blokes, all wearing balaclavas, drove by. It gave me such a shock. It was one of those moments when you try to yell but nothing comes out? That's what happened there to me. They drove past really slowly, put their windows down and pointed their fingers like guns towards us and then they drove off. It all happened so quickly and unexpectedly we didn't get any rego.

The next week, another doorman and I were standing on the door and it was quiet. I suggested to the other doorman that we bring the barriers in a bit closer to the door because wasn't that busy. So we did and within two minutes of bringing them in, a car came past the same way. Suddenly there were bullets firing out of the car and they put eight or nine bullet holes into the window of the hairdresser's next door. That was right where we had been standing only minutes before. Everything just happened so fast. All I remember was the noise of the guns going off. If we had not moved the barriers, the other guard and I would have felt the full force of those bullets. For about five minutes after they left, I just stood by the window were I would have been standing, staring. I was in shock. I would have been dead if we hadn't brought those barriers in closer.

Some others weren't so lucky. One patron who was coming out of the club got hit twice with the bullets and Levi the door host's mate Junior got a bullet in the stomach. Levi and I got scrapes on our legs from it. God was looking down on me that night. The cops never found out who did that but I don't know how hard they tried either. That's what shits me about the cops—if it had been one of their lot getting fired at they would have done everything to find that car and the people involved. Are you telling me that they couldn't look for the car using the street CCTV? That's why I always said the cops didn't care what happened that night. In a way, I reckon they were hoping one of us got hit. That would mean one less one of us for them to worry about. After that, the cops and the council were doing everything in their power to close DCM's down. The cops would be doing walk-throughs at least three or four times a night. Even when we were having a big event at the club they would come down and do a raid on the club and close it down with 1,000 plus people in there. One night, they closed us down and wanted to count every person in the club by doing a head count one by one as they came down the stairs from the club. They didn't realise that doing this would make the crowd get fired up. As 90 per cent of them would be peaking on their pills. When things like this happened the dance floor would have pills scattered all over the dance floor.

Is this it?

The cops in Oxford Street would never go out of their way to help us—they were probably hoping that we all got shot. After that night I watched the road carefully and checked out nearly every car that pulled up anywhere near the club. That taught me to always keep my eyes up above the footpath and to check out the road and any cars that went past.

Just after this happened I got a call from my grandad's sister, Peggy, and her husband Uncle George, from Liverpool. I knew it was serious because Peggy never rang me, especially while I was living in Australia. She said that my grandad was asking about what should happen to the house if something happened to him? The first thing I said was 'Nothing's going to happen to him so let's not talk about it.' But they wanted an answer for peace of mind. So I said that I didn't want him to sell it. The house meant a lot to me and I knew it had been my nan's pride and joy. I said out of respect to my nan and grandad I wanted it to stay a Cummins house, as it had been in the family since the 1920s. 'Tell him not to get rid of it,' I said.

Uncle George told me that Grandad was going to sign the house over to me. I was gob-smacked when he said that, but I said that I didn't want to talk about it. He understood that, but he wanted to put me in the picture to what was going on. I left it at that.

A few weeks later I got a call from my dad. He told me to come home to Liverpool, as my Grandad didn't have too much longer to live. So I flew to Liverpool, and spent some time with my dad, working at the club he had now in Southport called Fusion and playing football, and spending as much time as I could with my grandad.

Grandad was now being cared for in a home. These were my last memories of my grandad. I remember seeing Grandad on the bed and it wasn't him. It just wasn't the grandad I was used to. It was hard putting on a brave face for him. Every day I went to see him he was getting worse and I remember sitting on the edge of the bed with him and just giving him the biggest hug and telling him, 'I love ya Grandad.' He didn't say a word when I said that but I could see his eyes watered and that was enough to me that he knew. He got so bad that he couldn't eat anymore and to watch his body slowly switch off was upsetting. It got so upsetting that a few times I would run out of the building crying and screaming in the park for help for him. He put on a few smiles for me but by his body was shutting down. There was always hope at the back of my mind he would be okay and the next day I came to see him he would be sitting up and asking, 'Why am I here, take me home, Neil.' When he eventually passed away, me and Dad were coming home from his club in Southport, which he had opened just outside of Liverpool. It was about 2 in the morning and we got a phone call from where my grandad was staying, saying that his health had deteriorated and they didn't think he would make it to the morning so we should come over straightaway. It started to hit me that my grandad was leaving me and that I wouldn't see him again. I started yelling at my dad to drive faster so we could be there with him. My dad yelled back, 'Okay Neil, I'm fuckin' driving as fast as I can.' I didn't want him going with no-one around him. By the time we got to the home he had already passed away. I was devastated. I wanted one of us there so he could see us before he went. I remember pacing up and down the narrow halls not being able to breathe. I ran to his room not believing he had died and looking in and seeing him lying there all peaceful. I just kept saying, no, no, no. I went over and grabbed his hand and sat there with him for at least 30 minutes talking to him. I was asking him to wake up. I felt so empty: I'd just lost the most important person in my life.

The nurse told us that it looked like he was trying to stay alive to see us and only passed away half an hour before we got there. His hand was still warm but by the time I let go it was starting to get cold. Even while holding his hand his body was still moving which the first time I thought he had come back alive and I remember shouting for the nurse, but it was just the gases from his body. The funeral was hard. I needed to be left alone after it. I went and sat by my nan's grave for an hour or so just talking to her and my grandad. Hoping that they were back together. I slowly walked back to my grandad's house where everyone was waiting for me. I just sat on the back step and looked at the garden thinking of where my grandad was.

I flew back to Sydney and after about a week and a half I felt empty and lost. I was used to Grandad ringing me regularly and just talking to me about my life. I'd lost a great person and I felt lonely and alone.

In Sydney, DCM's was winding down. There were calls from residents and the gay community in Oxford Street to close it. There was a big petition delivered to the council about it. Straight clubs were not welcome on Oxford Street it seemed. Then a guy was caught with a semi-automatic in the back lane of DCM's, and the Council and police finally got their wish and shut it down.

Out of the blue, the phone rang and it was my dad's sister, Peggy. She told me that Dad had sold Grandad's house. He hadn't told anybody, there was no phone call to anybody—he just sold it. Everyone knew the house had been put in my name, but he'd sold it behind my back. I called Uncle George and he said that my dad had sold the house. He said your grandad wanted you to have the house and put it in your name Neil. After that happening, my dad and I didn't talk for a few years. I couldn't believe he had just sold it like he did. With so much history in that house, the only way to still feel connected to both my nan and grandad was through the house. Now there is no Cummins in Redington Road, Allerton, for the first time in over 80 years. It still upsets me what he did, but there's nothing I can do about it now. I wondered if Dad was jealous of the relationship I had with both my grandparents. They gave me everything I wanted. I never asked for anything: they'd just do it without me knowing sometimes. When Nan passed away, Grandad would send me money out and I would tell him I was okay, you don't need to send me money. But his answer would be, 'Your Nan would want you to have it,' or 'What am I going to do with it? It's just sitting in the bank doing nothing, so you might as well have it and spend it on something you need.' Grandad didn't like the banks and always thought the banks were taking his money so he would always take money out and keep bundles of cash rolled up in his socks in his cupboards.

While DCM's was going downhill, John sent me to look after a new venue called Havana nightclub on Oxford Street, right next door to the well-known gay pub called Stonewall. Really, it was the new venue for DCM's. For the first couple of weeks it was busy, but then the regulars started to go elsewhere. It had the same DJs and lights and lasers from DCM's, but it just didn't have the atmosphere. I think the place was too small, and there were no podiums. It's hard for a doorman to pick a crowd when the people just aren't coming to your venue. I sometimes had to let people I would never let in, as it was quiet and not busy like the old DCM's. We even started to close at 3am. I think the biggest problem was the gangs that started to come every week to Havana. It wasn't that they started to play up, they'd just put people off. The young kids didn't want to come anymore and I started to lose my good guards.

Then I started getting guards who had never worked at a nightclub before or just weren't guards you would use at a nightclub. I had one guard who had only just got his licence. He was 18 years old weighing in at 45 kilograms if he was lucky. What was I suppose to do with him? I put him upstairs to roam around, but he could never kick anyone out if they played up. He would come downstairs to the front door to tell me that he has asked a certain person to leave but they wouldn't. So I would have to go up and kick him out. If you're a doorman you have to have some presence about you and be able to handle yourself, otherwise go and work outside a bank. Havana's was like a sinking ship.

For a while, the cops didn't even know that we had moved DCM's up to Havana. They only realised when they saw the whole crew of doormen and staff. It was quite funny to see their faces when they figured it out. It was like we got one over them. The cops saw the club was struggling and started to give us a really hard time. We could do no right with them. They'd come past three or four times every night, just trying to get us on something to close us down. One Friday night, one copper was trying to arrest someone in the street, a building away from Havana. I was out on the street and could see he was having trouble. He was on his own and he had no back up. So I helped him out and got the guy to the ground for him. Did I get any thanks? Like hell I did. If I didn't help him that night he wouldn't have got the bloke or he might even have been hurt. After that I didn't go out of my way to help them. If they were just going to work against me then fuck 'em I say. Don't get me wrong, there were some good cops I had time for, but that was only a handful out 50.

I used to find it funny that the coppers thought I was a bikie. They thought they knew everything but they know nothing about what's really happening. So what if I was talking to a few known bikies outside the club? What they didn't realise was I was mostly telling them they couldn't come in and asking them to go back to their area! They were always trying to get me for something, it didn't matter what, they just wanted something on me.

As I had a good relationship with most bikie gangs, the gang members knew I would let them in if I could. It was respect at the end of the day. Even when situations would happen on Oxford Street and the cops would come down to ask questions, they'd think I see everything. But all I'm interested in is looking after my door, my guards and watching my back. Not what's going on down the footpath or in the next nightclub. There was one copper who had just joined the beat on Oxford Street and he was new to the force. I think he wanted all his colleagues to think that he was a good cop, but he caused a lot of trouble with his attitude. He thought he was a commando more than he was a copper from the way he spoke to me, my guards or patrons. One night he was totally out of order, being rude and aggressive towards me and my guards. I turned around to him and the cop in charge of the beat and said I don't want to talk to you guys anymore until I see someone higher than you guys. I told all my guards to not help or do anything for them unless their attitude changes. The area commander came down the next night and I told her what had happened. She said she wanted to work together like I wanted.

When I was on the doors at Havana I got a message from Marcel who worked at the door at the strip club DreamGirls. Had I heard the news? I rang Marcel and he told me that Fadi Ibrahim had been shot. My first words were 'FUCK OFF.' He said he didn't know how true it was, but that was the rumour. I tried calling Fadi's mobile to see if it was true, but there was no answer. I tried to get in touch with everyone to find out what had happened, but no-one knew anything. I ran upstairs to the office of Havana to see the manager of the club, Margaret, to see if she had heard. She hadn't heard anything and straight away she got on the phone to find out. When she confirmed it was true, I was in shock. I couldn't believe it. I had no desire to carry on working. All I kept wondering was how is my mate, how bad was it, is he okay? I knew nothing. I rang a mate to come pick me up. The door didn't matter to me anymore, nothing did.

Everyone around me knew I was upset about it and not knowing how bad he was, was doing my head in. I finally left work and went straight to the hospital but only the family was allowed in. He'd been shot five times. His girlfriend Shayda had been shot too, as they sat in his black Lamborghini outside his house in Castle Cove. He was in a coma for three weeks. I went the hospital with Dave and Adam Freeman, when he finally came around, but still only family were able to see him. But it was good to know he was out of danger. No-one was ever charged for that shooting. I caught up with Fadi as soon as he went home to his house and would hang out there a lot. Still to this day he is still paying for that night. Fadi went through hell and back with his body after the shooting and still is. Hopefully one day he will be back to normal and be the fit Fadi he once was.

That shooting set up a whole chain of events that led to allegations about me from police constable Jenna-Lee Hughes that I asked her to search the police database for information. She ended up with a prison sentence. A lot of cops are fascinated with the underworld scene and would ask me questions about what it was like. At the end of the day, I have no control over what anyone does in their spare time or while they're at work. For years I had a lot of friends in the police force from playing soccer to working in the industry, but that shouldn't stop them from being my mate. After that Jenna-Lee Hughes allegation, a lot of coppers I knew didn't talk to me anymore or even say hi. All because of who I am. They think I'm trouble, but really I was just a bodyguard and someone who looked after someone's venues.

By then, Havana had started to go downhill. There were a lot of fights and on a Friday night all the Asian gangs would turn up there as well—5Ts and Triads. One Friday night, the bikies and the Triads had a stand-off upstairs. I tried my best to calm the situation down but suddenly all hell had broken loose. Stools and and bottles were being thrown everywhere and people were getting launched down the stairs. It was all on—bikies, Lebanese and Asians all fighting. People trying to get out were getting knocked over. I tried to isolate the ringleaders and get them out of the venue and just push the first group nearest the door out of the building. Problem is that then they would hang around waiting for the others to come out. I only had six doormen on that night, with only two reliable ones and the rest were young first-timers. In the middle of it all, one doorman shouted at me, 'This is my first night on the doors. I've only done static work outside a bank.' What was I supposed to do with that?

A lot of organised gangs came to that club: Brothers for Life, the Auburn boys, all from the west of Sydney. Out of all the gangs I had to control the one I learnt you don't fuck with were the Triads. Having said that, they didn't want to make trouble, they just wanted to make money, while a lot of other gangs made too much noise and stood out. That's why cops were always on to them, but the Triads were pretty well organised and stuck together. The Bra Boys were hard to control when they were on the piss, but just like all the other gangs, it was the young people coming through the so-called ranks who were out of control. The old-school Bra Boys were respectful and I had a good relationship with Sunny and Koby Abberton and if any of their group messed up I would let them know. At the end of the day there is always someone who will give a certain gang or organised group a bad name and step out of line and fuck up. The bikie and gang scene at Havana was getting out of control and I couldn't do anything about it. In the end I'd given up. They killed that club for everyone.

There was one time when a few of the older boys came down to the club with some younger ones. Halfway through the night the older boys left and the younger ones stayed on. I went upstairs to check everything was okay. When the older boys had left I told them that the younger ones had to leave with them, but they say they could stay and they'd been told to behave. They didn't want them coming with them. You'd have some younger members thinking they had power now and they didn't have to listen to me. There was a few of them, believe me, but they were soon put back in their place. As I have said before I didn't, care who you were, if you came to my venue you went by my rules or see ya later.

I got upstairs and there were two boys left by the bar with a heap of drinks just for two guys. They had a few girls around them. I went over and asked them if everything was alright and one of them knew of me and said 'Yeah, Neil, we're good. The girl behind the bar has been giving us free drinks.' I asked her why she was doing that and she said they kept dropping so many names that she thought they had to get free drinks. I told her that unless they paid for them they weren't getting free drinks. I told the boys that they had to start paying for their drinks. They said sure.

After about an hour, the manager asked me to come upstairs. He told me the boys at the bar were paying for their drinks with forged notes. They had spent over four hundred dollars with fake $50 notes. I went over to the one who knew me and asked him to come up to the office. He followed me as he knew something was up. Now his brother was quite high up in Notorious, so when I got him in the office I first asked him if he was having a good night. He said 'Yeah, Neil, I'm having a top night. Didn't you see all the chicks we've got?' I asked him if he was paying for his drinks.

'Yeah, Neil, look I've got money,' he said and with that he put more fake $50s in front of me. When he did that I asked him if this was all his money.

'Yeah,' he said. I asked him again, 'Are you sure this is all your money?'

'Yeah,' he said. 'I had over $1,000 all in $50 notes.' When he said that I gave him the biggest right hand to the face, dropping him to the floor. Then I slapped him again.

He shouted at me. 'Do you know who I am?'

I said 'Yes, I know who you are. Do you know who I am?' and hit him again.

'Listen here, you little cunt. Who do you think you are coming down here with the boys and knowing who owns this venue and spending nearly $500 in fake notes. Do you know who you are ripping off?'

By then he was calmer, 'How many notes does your mate have on him?'

'Nothing, it's just me.'

So I called Samoan Dave and told him what had happened and that these boys had just put everyone all on show by doing this. Dave lost it and said to me he would sort it out. He told me to kick him out and said he would deal with him later. I kicked him out but we kept the notes. At least he got a good hiding for doing it. He was so lucky he was the brother of one of the Notorious boys otherwise there would have been no phone call, just a flogging.

11

Bodyguard

While I was working at DCM's, John Ibrahim offered me a night job working during the week in the Cross at DreamGirls and Porky's Nite Spot. I started looking after the escort girls from 9pm until 4am, to make sure all the guys paid up and that the girls were safe in the venue. Not that the girls were my cup of tea and I reckon most of the time the guys were so pissed they probably couldn't see what they were like. Their 'mother hen' was a big, blonde busty woman called Anne. She and I were always having a joke and she knew everybody who came in and out. At first, while working there, she looked out for me and always said she would tell John how good I was at my job. These girls made so much money! Doctors and lawyers would go there and stay with the girls for five or six hours and spend over $5,000. I couldn't bloody believe it. I reckon the person who made the most out of the lot of them was an Asian guy who had a full sex change to become a girl. Believe me, you couldn't tell. So many girls would come and go while I was working there, young and old. Girls would come looking for work from as far as Brisbane and Melbourne. Some would need the money and the rest would just be passing through. DreamGirls was a good place to work and a good night out. It wasn't just a strip club. It was more of a nightclub as well. It had a party vibe and everyone who went there could enjoy themselves and let their hair down. The staff were cool to work with as well and I made a lot of friends working there.

Two doormen, Marcel and Jimmy, had been there for years. They'd spruik in the street to bring in the crowd for DreamGirls and get guys in for Porky's. They had seen everything at the Cross, real wheelers and dealers, and we got on great. Marcel's wife came from Liverpool. Jimmy always said he wanted to be as big as me, but most of all they had my back covered, if needed. Even though I never needed it. You could trust both of them to be there for you and they were loyal. When I wasn't around they would always keep me informed about what was going on. I always told them to call me at any time of the night if they needed me to kick someone out or if someone turned up at the venue who shouldn't be there.

Old Frank Amante owned both places. I met Frank in 2000 at a New Year's Eve party before I knew anyone in the Kings Cross circle. Frank is the nicest guy you will ever meet and he became a father figure for me while I was working at the Cross. I can honestly say I loved Frank because I did. I would do anything for that bloke. While I was working at his joints, he was in and out of hospital for his liver and at one stage we didn't think he was going to pull through, but he did. To me, Frank is the godfather of the Cross.

Everyone was always coming past Porky's to sell stuff on the street to the punters. If you needed anything from clothes to laptops they would have it. There were so many characters in the Cross from all different backgrounds. They all stood and sat in the same place all the time, day after day. I even had one person come past the door and ask me if I needed some clothes. I thought maybe he meant some sportswear or industry clothes. But he said he'd just taken them off the clothes line.

'Who's line, your line?' I asked.

'Yeah, you want them?' He must have been desperate for the cash because I felt like saying look mate those are clothes that even the charity shops won't touch—they were just rags.

Then there was Archie, who was the manager of Love Machine, the strip club across the road. He was a nice bloke. He was like a newspaper—he knew everything that was going on in the Cross. The only problem I had with him was that he was an Everton supporter. Two other people who worked at Love Machine, who I can't forget were Sabby and Big Billy. Sabby was spruiker on the door. There is no-one in this world like Sabby. He had the kindest heart, but could talk some bullshit too. He was about four-foot tall, with gold jewellery everywhere you can think of all over him. He would talk himself up so much that I think he thought he was the King of the Cross. He was a lookalike for Danny DeVito and he would always have a story to tell you. Then there was Big Billy, who would be inside the venue if anyone fucked up. He'd also be in the cash booth where people had to pay before they go in.

One night, a middle-aged Turkish guy was in the club and just sat by himself all night. When he went into a private show with one of the girls I got a call to remove him because he was touching the girls. It was a strictly 'look but don't touch' kind of show.

I told him he had to leave, but he wouldn't get out. So I grabbed his arm to force him out and he growled at me. I kept nudging him towards the stairs to the exit when he pulled a knife on me and started shouting at me. I launched at him, hitting him in the face until he dropped the knife. Finally Jimmy and Marcel came down and Marcel kicked the knife away from him, and then started to shout at me to, 'Calm down Neil, just calm down.' I hate knives. It doesn't matter how big or small the knife is, they all do the same damage.

One Sunday night outside DreamGirls, there was a bloke who had just got out of jail. He was known in the Cross as Smiley. I was standing outside on the doors with Big Fadi. John Ibrahim was downstairs in DreamGirls with a few friends. Smiley kept walking past and looking at the door out of the corner of his eye. He looked like he was up to something. I didn't trust him, but I didn't say anything to Fadi, as I wanted to see what he might do. With John downstairs, I had to be careful who went down. All of a sudden Smiley made a dash for the entrance to go downstairs. As he did he pulled a gun out from the inside pocket of his jacket. I quickly launched myself at him not even thinking of the gun. All I had in my mind was John downstairs. I threw him against the wall in the stairwell, with the gun pointing everywhere. I grabbed his hand with the gun in it and kept head-butting him until he dropped it. As soon as he dropped it, I launched him down the stairs and Big Fadi took over from there while I went back upstairs. I knew everything was okay and I'd done my job. I don't even reckon John knew what happened that night. I never found out what Smiley was about to do either.

Another night, I was on duty at Porky's during the week and the rumour went around that John was in the club. He found me and asked me to walk around the Cross with him as he didn't have Tongan Sam with him that night. There was an afterparty downstairs in Dragonfly for Beyoncé and he wanted to check it out and see it was all going okay. I couldn't believe it. This was a massive opportunity for me, and showed that he trusted me to look after him. I knew I had to be switched on. To become a bodyguard was a huge goal. I sooo didn't want to fuck up.

Dragonfly was packed. You couldn't move. John walked across the bar and sat down at his usual table in the corner. Then he asked me to take his girlfriend Chelsea into the VIP section on the other side of the club, where Beyoncé and her crew were partying. When I walked Chelsea over, one of Beyoncé's bodyguards, a big African-American dude, stopped us and told me Chelsea couldn't get in. I yelled at him. 'This is the owner's girlfriend!' At that point he pushed me out the way and told me again that she was not coming in. So I pushed him back and he went to run at me but was stopped. John came over quickly yelling at me to calm down. 'Relax, Neil' he shouted. 'You can't knock out one of Beyoncé's own bodyguard's!' I backed down.

That night I didn't know where to stand and what to do. John was not like the people I had looked after before. I was star-struck. I keep thinking, 'Oh my god, I am actually here doing this.' But I lost my cool, so I went back to Porky's. I told my mates on the door what had happened, and Marcel and Jimmy patted me on the back. 'You are good to look after John,' they said and encouraged me not to give up. If John wanted me he would come and ask me again. I wasn't going to push it. I wanted to earn my stripes.

Havana was coming to the end of its run, as the club was dying every week. Even though we had tried everything to get people to come there, it wouldn't be long before the club would close. I was standing on the door and got a message. It was John. I would often get messages from him as he would see how things were going at Havana's while he was out and about, but he never visited. Or I would message him to see if a certain person could come in the club or, if he was in the Sunday paper, I would let him know as the newsagent was next door to Havana.

He messaged me saying, 'Now Havana is closing, what do you want to do?'

I texted back straight away. 'I want to just look after you and when you're not around just look after the venues.'

In two minutes he replied with one word that would change my life: 'Done'.

That was it. It was that quick. All that hard work had paid off. I had done it at last. I had climbed that ladder at last. My next goal was to drive him around and be with him 24/7. I knew Tongan Sam was also there and I respected that. I had got the respect that I wanted from John. I was capable of looking after him, instead of waiting on doors at the venues. I stood on the door for the rest of the night with the biggest smile on my face, but didn't tell anyone, even though I wanted to.

The next weekend, I started in my new role. I would wait for John at the door of the Piano Room, a new club that was part of the Tradmark Hotel, for his car to pull up. He would handshake everyone who was there and then I would follow him around the Cross all night. We would mostly hang outside Porky's on the main strip of Kings Cross. He would walk through all his nightclubs to show his presence and to check up on things and I would follow him and watch every car and every person that came near him. No weapons though. Didn't need to, didn't want to. The only guns I used were my biceps! I had my eyes and ears and my body, and that was enough for him and enough for me.

I would wear all black—black jeans, shoes and T-shirt so it was easy to move. I never wore anything tight. I wasn't on my own, there were several of us. Tongan Sam would turn up and we'd work together. Sometimes a few other guys would also work—Ash, Richie and Turkish Mick, although he was more of a going out mate for John. I don't even think Mick could fight.

We would always make our way to Porky's when John arrived at the Cross and go and see Frank Amante who owned Porky's and DreamGirls. He was like a father figure to everyone and mostly went everywhere with John. John looked out for Frank. Even though Frank had been through a lot with his health, he was always at Porky's rain, hail or shine. Standing outside Porky's while John would talk and catch up with people, I would watch everything. I didn't even like it sometimes when people would come up to John and ask for photos. Anyone could do anything at any time. They don't have to look suspicious. Plus the footpath on a Saturday night is packed with people, sometimes shoulder to shoulder busy. Sometimes you would think, is it this person or that one who might start something. Then there are the cars. We would stand on the edge of the pavement and on a Saturday night cars would be bumper to bumper. Even when we were walking, John was a fast walker, so you had to keep up with him and he would always lead. Watching everyone coming towards us, I would think any one of those people could just do something quickly and run off and be lost in the crowd. John's not scared of anything and he couldn't care less if there is a hit on his life. Sometimes he would go places without anyone around him. Sometimes I would be over-protective, but that was me. I was there to do a job and look after a mate. Even when I wasn't needed I would be thinking to myself, I should be there, because there is always that thing in the back of your head saying 'What if?' Even if I did just have a drink with John at a venue or even at his place, I was in work mode. I could never relax around him like I could with his brothers Fadi and Michael. I think I had got so used to being switched on around him that it was hard to switch off. I remember back in the DCM days a fight broke out upstairs in the house room. I was doing a walk through and John was upstairs. We both went to sort it out. We cleaned all the guys up in the fight, but I was also trying to watch John's back to that no-one got him. Even during the summer when we were both down at Bondi Beach, I felt I had to switch on to work mode from relax mode. I didn't trust anybody when John was around me. Then again I know if we were out drinking and I was a bit pissed he would pull one of my mates aside and tell them to watch over me. I think he thought I was a loose cannon when I drank.

I became better friends with John's brothers Fadi and Michael. Maybe not better friends, but I could certainly be much more relaxed around them. Maybe it was because Fadi and Michael were more down-to-earth than John. Fadi would always tell me to come over to his place or come out with him, but he would always go out on a Saturday night when I was working. With Michael I was just starting to get close and have a friendship like I had with Fadi when he got locked up. Sam tended to hang out at Parramatta with his own boys. The place I partied at week in, week out with all the boys was the Swiss Grand at Bondi Beach. It was the best place and it used to go off. It was a day club on the top of the hotel roof. The atmosphere was unbelieveable. People were dancing on tables and chairs in shorts and the girls were just hanging out there in bikinis. It was like being in Ibiza in the south of Spain. It was mad. I was there every Sunday without fail until it stopped. It took all the trade away from the Ivy Pool in the city, which was trying to do the same but it was nowhere near as good. Everyone was in party mood. Why would you go Ivy Pool when you can party at Swiss and look out over Bondi Beach?

I used to finish up working on a Saturday morning and get home by about 9am to my unit in Bondi were I was living with my mate, Lincoln. I'd have a shower, get some breakfast and go down to the Swiss at 11am. Then it was party all day and all night. Lincoln wouldn't go out on a Friday or Saturday night so he could save himself for our all-day Sunday.

The first time I went there I thought of Fadi straight away. This was his kind of place. When I was working for John, I just had my mind on the job. It was important to keep all my eyes and ears open for any trouble. That's what I had been trained to do. I never drank or got on the pills when I was walking the Cross with John. Lots of people have asked me if I needed to do that to stay awake. But I didn't. I just naturally got energy from my work. And John is such a magnetic person to be around, you get energy from that. There's always something happening, someone to talk to. All the people we met and worked with at the Cross were interesting, they always had some story to tell. So when it came to time out for me, I partied hard. And there was never anyone better for me to party with than my mates.

Fadi was a party animal too and we got to go out a lot. When I was with Fadi I could relax, I was off duty. So thinking he would love the Swiss Grand, I called Fadi to tell him about it to get him down there. 'Pool party on roof top of Swiss Grand Bondi,' I said down the phone. That was all it took. He was off the phone and there within half an hour. 'Wait for me out the front, Neil,' Fadi would say to me. Every week we would text each other just the words 'Swiss Grand'. That was our sign and we knew we were on for Sunday. Sometimes it got pretty wild and there were always other guys down there drinking a lot as well. The venue had it all under control, and there wasn't much trouble. Problem with Fadi is that he was a bit like Lee, my mate back in Liverpool—people knew who he was. They knew he was an Ibrahim, and John and Sam's brother. So that attracted people to take him on and make a crack at him or even take him on for a fight. I would often step in and calm it down and pull him out, but it wasn't always possible to stop what someone else was thinking.

One guy was determined to pick a fight with Fadi. He kept egging him on and, being a dickhead, saying stuff to him when he went to the bar, and making in-your-face gestures to him. Fadi cracked and took a swipe and then it was on. We cleaned the guy up, but I knew it would get back to John. He didn't like Fadi making a scene in public. He liked everything to go quietly under the radar. And he didn't want me to be involved in anything either. Fadi knew it would get back to John as well.

The next time I saw John, he asked me 'What's going on at the Swiss Grand?' He'd heard me and Fadi were running amuck together and then there had been some fight on Sunday. Somebody had told him before I could get the chance! I said some guy was a dickhead to Fadi and he cracked. John said that Fadi and I weren't a good mix, and said we needed to stop partying with each other until we could get a grip on it. That was it. We were barred from partying together. Which is quite funny when you think about it. I messaged Fadi, and asked him if he had spoken to John. Straight away he said yes and texted back in big letters in a message 'WE

ARE BARRED!' I cracked up. I texted to Fadi 'It's the last Swiss Grand this Sunday.' He replied 'I know, but I can't go.' I wrote back 'Fuck! My partner in crime can't come.'

That Sunday I was there at the Swiss Grand and then John came down as well with a few other people. It was great to be there with John and his mates. Everyone from the Kings Cross circle was there and we were all having the best time. Dave Freeman was there with his brother Adam, which was great. But I really wanted Fadi there as well—he was my party mate. After a few drinks I got up a bit of Dutch courage and asked John if Fadi could come down. I knew he was sitting at home on his own wishing he was with us. John said no at first. I tried again, saying 'It's the last Swiss, John.' Then John said 'If he comes out you will have to look after him. He's your responsibility, not mine.'

'That's fine with me,' I said and thanked him. I called Fadi straight away.

'Get changed and head down to the Swiss.'

'I can't! John's barred me.'

'I've sorted it with John. You can come! So hurry up.'

Fadi was there in 10 minutes, dressed to the nines and ready to party. By that time everyone else was there. We partied till midnight. That was the best night out with Fadi and me dancing on tables. Great memories!

There was another time that Fadi and I got into shit for again doing something together, but this time for different reasons. While John was overseas I was hanging with Fadi most days and just as I finished at the gym one day I got a call from Fadi to meet him outside the gym. Straight away I asked if everything was okay and he said, 'Yes mate, just need to see you.' I told him I would be there in half an hour. We met at the coffee shop around the corner. As soon as I got there he said 'You will like what I have to say Neil'.

'Yeah,' I said, 'Well tell me'.

He asked me to go with him to Westfield Bondi Junction to see someone. The person was a friend of the circle but I had heard as well that he had been talking shit about me a few weeks earlier, so that's why Fadi asked if I would like to come. Fadi was like that with me, he would gee me up. Fadi was only going to meet up and have a chat with him, nothing special, but he knew I would like to maybe tag a long after what this bloke had been saying about me. We went there and Fadi had a chat with him and I was going to let it go, but he said something smart about me, just as we were leaving. It straightaway pushed my buttons. I went straight up to him and went off at him. He mouthed off again and I just grabbed him and pushed him towards the barrier on the third level of the shopping centre and put his head over it, telling him if he wants to start I will gladly start on him. Fadi grabbed me and yelled at me to let him go, thinking I was about to knock his head off. I did and walked off. When John got back from overseas he was told what had happened and pulled me aside and asked me what happened. I told him and told him I thought I was doing the right thing looking out and being there for Fadi while he was overseas, but I was told not to do anything like that again unless I contacted John first.

My other party mate was Lincoln. We were sharing a flat in Bondi, and if I wasn't working on a Wednesday night, we'd go to the Eastern Hotel instead of going out on the weekend. One night we were there until late and one guy got into an argument with Lincoln. Before I realised what was going down, Lincoln had suddenly been king hit from the side and was knocked down to the floor. With his mouth bleeding, I said 'What happened, who did it?' Lincoln told me to leave it because he didn't want any hassle, but I couldn't. Lincoln was like my brother and my best mate. He'd smashed his nose on the way down and there was blood all over his face. There was no chance of me leaving it. I asked one of the guys standing around who did it. They pointed out a guy to me, standing at the bar with two of his mates.

I walked over as cool as you like and just went fuck off in his face with my right hand. Remember I don't punch any more, only slap. I still reckon my slap is better than any punch. The guy dropped like a bag of shit to the floor. His two mates came at me, and I shouted at them to bring it on, stirring them up. 'Just try it!' I shouted to the guy on the floor. 'You'll think twice next time before you fuckin' mess with someone, won't you dickhead.' He got up and ran behind the bar and wouldn't come out until I left. The doorman from downstairs came up and shouted at me.

'What's going on, Neil?'

'Listen, I'm not going anywhere until this guy gets downstairs and out of this place.'

'Who?'

I looked at the dickhead who had crawled behind the bar. 'I'm not coming out unless he goes,' he shouted, terrified.

The doorman looked at me, as if to say well what do you think I should do next?

'If he is not out of this place in 10 minutes, I'm coming to get him out,' I said and walked out of the Eastern and stood out on the pavement. Lincoln's nose was fucked. I wasn't going anywhere.

The two doormen kept coming over to me and walking backwards and forwards from the doors to me on the pavement, trying to calm me down. 'Neil, come on mate, go home. Get him another day. It's time to call it quits mate.'

'It was him who started it,' I said. 'I'm the one out here on the pavement but it was him who started it in the first place.'

'Come on mate, let's leave it for now, let's call it a day.'

'I could have the biggest crew down here right now to sort this out you know,' I said. 'So go and get him and get him out so I can have a drink without someone hitting my mate.'

I never used John's name in front of anyone, but they all knew who I was and who I worked for. That got them scared. But I'm not really like that, and all I wanted was the person who hit my mate, outside. On the pavement. Now.

They kept me talking and kept me out of the club until it was closing time. So I waited, and then he came down the stairs, with all his mates around him.

'I'm going to get you, you dog,' I called out to him. 'You think your boys will stop me? I'll drop them all.'

I kept walking all the way to the top of the road hoping to get a clean shot at him with my left, but all his mates were around him making sure I couldn't get to him. As he got to the turn in the road his mates in front thought he was turning right to go down the street but he went straight-ahead. That was my chance and I gave him a big upper cut and dropped him.

153

The Muscle

I was barred from the Eastern for six weeks. Even though they let the other guy and his mates in I was the one shut out. I was so angry. John said I should leave it, and go somewhere else. He didn't go to the Eastern anyway. But I couldn't see that they could let that dickhead in and bar me. It didn't make sense. I went down there on a Wednesday on my own and went off at the doormen about it. One of the doorman could see I was getting pissed off and kicked out the guy and barred him for a week. He told me to come back in a week and he'd let me back in. So the next week Lincoln and I went back for a drink. Everyone watched as we walked in, but we weren't there to cause trouble. It changed my opinion of the place and we stopped going there after that.

I was once offered a job by Justin Hemmes. He runs the Ivy in George Street with all its bars and VIP room and a pool bar, where I would go if I did get a night off. He ran the Merivale House in George Street and the Hemmes family owns and operates about 10 Sydney venues and a heap of restaurants, bars and hotels like the Establishment and Tank nightclub. Also a music company called Jam Music. Someone told me the VIP booths have a minimum spend of $2,500. Well I never paid that. I would always get the booths for free, thanks to having friends on the inside there. I used to love going to the Ivy. Not for the venue, but because everyone in there was up themselves badly. They all think they are somebody, but really they were nobodies. Half the crowd in there went to DCM's and even some of them tried to get in but I would never let them, but they get into Ivy because they put a pair of dress pants on and a collared shirt. Shows how strict I was. Everyone in there thinks they are rich or have a bit of cash and flash it around to impress people, but really it's their whole pay from that week in their wallet and until next payday they will be broke. It was so fake in there. Even the girls who went there were fake. All dressed up looking for that rich guy with their fake tan on, short skirts and fake Gucci bags, thinking they looked like a celebrity, but really they worked in some retail store. It was funny to watch. One night I took all the doormen from the Cross there. All big Islanders, you can just imagine what that looked like. We ran amuck. They had never been in there before and I don't think they would have got in if I hadn't have taken them that night.

I had a good reputation in the business and was always seen around the Cross. Justin Hemmes asked me to work for him in 2006. I didn't even think twice about it and I turned him down. I was happy with where I was working. It wasn't about the money or the place or the prestige or anything. I respected John and working for him was, to me, the peak of my career. I enjoyed every day working for him and the crew that were part of the business. And on top of that I am an incredibly loyal person. I never leave to go anywhere until I am pushed. I stay until the end. I will fight for my mates and my brothers until I am the last one standing. I could never leave to go just anywhere. There was only one person who could have tempted me away from John. My dad. If he had said come and work for me then, yes I would have left John. But everyone knew I was part of the furniture with John and I wouldn't go anywhere. I'm that kind of person. I was loyal to John and his family. So loyal, that in 2009 I nearly got a tattoo to show my loyalty.

John knew everybody and everybody knew him. To all of John's close mates he was known as 'Sexy' not John. Good nickname—hey, it suits him. Because of Sam's links to the bikies, there were a lot of ex-bikies or members who would come and hang out with us. Mark Judge used to hang out with us, and then he got embroiled in the media with Jodi Gordon, the star of *Home and Away*, and got stabbed in Bellevue Hill. Stuff like that I didn't really bother about. Okay, he thinks he is a somebody, but I didn't really care. Problem was when some of the guys and their mates partied, they partied hard. I was often the only one who could tell them when it was time to call it a night. Plus most of these guys only came down to the club to hang off John and try to look good. Even some, without mentioning any names, would try to be like him or even try to outdo him. The only problem was John didn't have to try to look good or be someone else. I never had time for any of those guys talking shit every week, telling me what they had or what they were buying. I didn't give a shit. John had a nice Range Rover, then all of a sudden everyone was driving Range Rovers in a way to say 'look at me'.

As John's bodyguard, I was a professional. My job was to look after John and keep him safe. For me, it was that simple. I just looked after John and kept my nose clean. Don't get me wrong, I was sometimes offered deals to let people into the clubs, people I knew who were dealing drugs, but I didn't. The only time I would take stuff was when I said to a few mates who came to DCM's that I would get them in for free if they would bring me some free steroids. And they did. I couldn't believe it when they turned up at the door with a bag full of steroids for me. I couldn't stop laughing. Christmas all at once. I was told to stop drug dealers and to keep them out and I knew I would lose my job if I let them in. I would never want to disrespect John. He has an amazing talent and charisma in the Cross. Everyone who comes across him never forgets that they have had that experience. Working for someone like John meant I had the power to go anywhere and get in anywhere in the Cross and in the clubs in the city and in Oxford Street. Everyone knew me and knew who I was. I could walk into any restaurant and would immediately be given a good table. It gave me a lot of status and I got VIP treatment wherever I went. Sometimes I would take my mates out with me to places and we'd just walk in and we would get shouted drinks all night by owners, managers and promoters. Even when I went up to Surfers in Queensland for holidays, people knew who I was and would invite me to their venues and be looked after all night. I would even be invited to VIP functions around the city or to the races.

When I was with John I didn't feel that I could talk to him about my life and our families. I would have liked to, and we got on really well when we were working. But it was hard for me to connect to him. I was focused on my work all the time. I couldn't relax—it would only take a second for me to let my guard down and someone could take a swipe at him. I think he noticed that a lot. He would say 'Relax, Neil' but I couldn't. He would always look out for me though. He looks after people who work for him. 'What's happening with you, Neil. Are you okay?'.

'Yeah, all good,' would be my standard answer. I didn't want to burden him with my life or what I was going through. So we wouldn't take up a conversation. Sometimes late at night we would go to Piano Room on Darlinghurst Road, another one of his venues. It's a place where it's easy to relax and kick back. The furnishings are all really lush and it's got this bar like a New York cocktail bar from the 1920s. That's where John would go if he wanted to be on his own. Sometimes I thought it would be good to talk to him there, but it just didn't feel right. I could relax more with Fadi and have a good time. Maybe it was because I wasn't working for him. John knew that I was totally loyal to him and that I always would be. I just wish I had opened up to him more. I have been asked so many times whether I would take a bullet for him and the answer was always yes. That's the truth, I would. I wouldn't let anyone touch John. I was very protective of him, even though I knew he was okay and could look after himself if needs be. I didn't care how big the person was or who he was I wouldn't have let any person get with in two yards of him. I even turned up at the airport when he was going away on holiday, just to make sure he was okay while checking in for his flight. The only thing I wouldn't do for him is carry a weapon, even if he asked me to do it. It's just not my style. I think we are similar, John and me, and that's why neither of us ever opened up. The one thing that John did enjoy me doing was dancing when I was on a night with him. It used to crack him up when I was dancing.

My mates were egging me on to get on TV. Maybe they thought I would be good-enough looking for a part! I wouldn't have minded being on the TV, so I auditioned to be a gladiator on the show *Gladiator* on Channel 7 in 2008. It's the ultimate test of physicality and a lot of the guys are so pumped for a massive competition. I was fighting fit and I reckoned I could take them all on. I did really well at the auditions and got to the last 20. I could tell that they liked me. They had you doing chin-ups for a minute and hold onto the bar, star jumps and sprint tests. Then they tested you on the gladiator games and I had to climb up to the top of the arena and let myself go. I had flashback memories of the balconies on the Gold Coast and had to get over a fear of heights that I had recently developed. So I just jumped! I can tell you that if I had stayed up there too long I wouldn't have done it. They liked me, and said I could be a possible contender. So they gave me heaps of forms to fill in and return to them. When I filled in the form it came down to the work experience. Current job? Doorman and bodyguard. Employer? John Ibrahim. I gave it back to them and well, as soon as I put that form in, I got a phone call from them to say they were sorry but they couldn't take me on. I was devastated.

I would go to Hugos Lounge in Kings Cross, fo nights out sometimes with Mariana. But they wouldn't let me in because of who I was. They were scared in case I started trouble in there with someone who may have been from a rival gang. It was also because of the size of me. It took a while for them to like me. For ages, they hated me coming there. There were a few times when I have gone and put it on them for the way they have treated me. They told me at one stage that I was barred, but didn't give me a reason why. I remember going to the door asking for the manager who barred me to come to the door but he never would cause he was too fuckin' shit-scared. It was hard, too, for some of the doormen there at the time as they all knew me. They would say he won't come to the door because he thinks you're going to go off at him. I would never go off at the doormen they were just doing their job and I knew them too. Just weak blokes like the manager hide inside making the doormen do the dirty work for him. At one point, the cops were called to stay near Hugo's in case I turned up, he was that scared. He wouldn't even come to the phone when I called Hugo's Lounge to speak to him. I remember getting a message through to him telling him to sort this and tell me why I'm barred or I would sort it out the next time I saw him walking in the street. Within a week I was allowed back in. I remember him standing at the top of the stairs to the entrance shitting himself when he saw me coming in and apologising for the misunderstanding. He walked me in and gave me a booth and a drink card for the night.

The Kings Cross cops hated me and were always watching me. I don't really know why—didn't they have anything better to do? Maybe it was because of me being so clean. They were always trying to pin something on me. But they couldn't. I was as clean as a whistle. They had tried hassling me on the doors at DCM's and now they saw me as one of John's bodyguards.

I remember one cop who had been around since I worked Soho/Yu. He used to be the licensing cop at the time. He walked past me while at the Cross and stopped and said, 'Neil Cummins, how are you? It's been a long time since I've seen you.' I remembered him straight away and gave him a grin. He asked me what I was doing up at the Cross that night. I told him just hanging out. He said, 'You've come a long way since your Yu days.' He told me he remembered me as a good doorman, who did a good job and kept to himself, but now he'd heard I looked after Mr John Ibrahim. 'I was hoping that wasn't true as I thought you were better than that, Mr Cummins,' he said.

'Everyone has their own opinion,' I replied.

'I thought you would have gone up in the world not down.'

I smiled and said, 'But I have, I'm always in the paper now, aren't I?'

With that he said, 'Well, I need to check you.' I asked what for.

'To make sure you're not carrying any weapons or things that you're not supposed to be carrying.'

I started laughing and said, 'Have you ever known me to carry anything?'

He said, 'No, but you weren't working for you-know-who back then.' So he put me against the wall outside Porky's and patted me down.

I've never had a record and I don't intend to get one. They called me into the Kings Cross Police Station and tried to charge me for an assault on a guy in Wollongong. I said you what? I had no idea what they were talking about. They said they had a witness. When we were in court, it all fell apart when the person who said I assaulted him admitted that the cops were feeding him information about me and pushing pictures of me in front of him at the police station. So the case was dropped. Even while I was in court that day the police had intelligence on me for being the main supplier of cocaine into Wollongong. I was in shock. I even looked at the cop who had brought the information to court and he even looked at me to say, I don't know where they get their info from. I have had a lot of things thrown at me: bikie, prostitution, weapons, drug supplier and standover man. Nothing stuck. But where were they getting this information? It was clearly not true.

Another cop in Kings Cross came up to me one night while John was talking to some people and took me aside. 'I've watched you, Neil, grow from a doorman that nobody knew to now somebody who everybody knows about for the wrong reasons. It's a pity for you.' But that's their opinion.

12

Breakdown

Even though I liked my job, by the end of 2008 I wasn't happy. I particularly wasn't happy in my marriage to Tiffani. I was changing. I was starting to get stressed out and I was having a hard time with stress at work and at home. There was a lot of responsibility on my shoulders. There was a lot of shit going on with rival bikie gangs that the Ibrahim family and myself were all trying to stay out of. I was getting constantly harassed by the police and it was getting on my nerves.

My marriage with Tiffani had hit rockbottom. I wanted out. I felt strangled by our marriage. It was clear that we were from two very different places. I'm not a bikie and I'm not a standover man. I worked as a professional, and even though some of the people I worked for were in the underworld, that wasn't my part in it. I did my job and came home.

But I felt Tiffani was always judging me and we argued about morals all the time. I felt I could never have a laugh or joke as I was always being judged. I love to dance and when I do I take up the whole dance floor. But we would go out and I couldn't relax enough to even dance. It got to the point where I would tell Tiffani that I was working, but instead I would hang out with Lincoln or at the Cross with a few of the doormen and then go home.

I partied a lot with drugs back then. At one point I would go out and have just coke and not as many drinks as I would have normally. I could get coke and pills as easily as if I was going through a McDonald's drive-thru. Drugs were always on tap for me whenever I wanted them and I can say I have never paid for my coke or my pills. They were always given to me as a thank you for looking after someone, looking out for someone, getting someone into a nightclub or just because of who I was. If I ever went to clubs and I wanted a line I would rack up there and then. I hated going into the toilets to rack up. It was dirty and at the end of the day what were they going to do, throw me out? I don't think so. But I didn't make it noticeable. I remember one night out when all my mates and I were all in a hotel before going out, we put all the bags of coke together and made one big fuckin' line on the kitchen bench. You had to see how much of the line you come snort in one go. That was crazy times.

There was also another drug I couldn't get enough of and that was steroids. They are a big part of my life. When I was on them I felt so good and calm. When off them, I was a cranky fucker. I started taking steroids back in 1999. I just thought I would give them a go. The results were out of control and when you have never used them before you can see why people want more of them. That was me. I started off small, but by 2004 I was well into them. I would start work on the doors with about 10 dinabol steriods in my pocket and by the end of the shift they would be all gone.

By 2007 I was popping 10 dinabolts a day and also having 6 ml injections every second day. I did that for three months straight. At one stage I even injected my chest. I was addicted. I wanted to be big and when I got to the size I wanted, I wanted to be bigger. I was 135 kilograms at one stage—all muscle—but that wasn't good enough. If a t-shirt was loose on me I would pop three or four dinabols at once or have an injection. I would look in the mirror and wouldn't see what everyone else could see. It played on my mind. It took a long time to get my head around it. Now I'm a lot better, but I still want to be bigger.

My daughter was the only thing making me happy. I would take her out to the park for hours to get out of the house during the day. I didn't feel I could just walk out, as I wanted to keep contact with my beautiful daughter, Lillian.

While Tiffani was out at a function one night I couldn't breathe. I had pins and needles and I was in a cold sweat. My mate Scottie rushed me to hospital and they kept me in for two nights while they checked on my heart. I wasn't having a heart attack, and I didn't have a stroke either. The doctor said it was stress and I should take it easy. When I got home, Tiffani didn't seem to be bothered about it. The only solution for me was to just hang out with my mates and try to work it all out, but that seemed to make it worse for her. She didn't want me hanging out with anyone who didn't have a girlfriend or a partner. She didn't like me going to the gym either, so that was out. I started to feel really alienated and down.

Close friends and family could see how miserable and down I was. They told me that, no matter what, Lillian would always be my daughter. Nobody could change that. So I made up my mind, packed my bags and moved out to my mate Lincoln's place in Bondi. My work became even more the focus of my life—it was the only way I could get a good feeling about myself. And when I had time off I partied even harder with the boys to try to forget about my disastrous marriage. A few days after I moved in I just went for a walk on my own, thinking about how much I missed my daughter and wondering what I was doing in my life, what I had become. I started contemplating suicide.

It wasn't the first time that suicide had crossed my path. My dad had tried to take his own life at my grandparents' house when I was about 10 years old. It was around the time of my parents' separation and Dad locked himself in the front room of my nan's house and took a bottle of sleeping pills. Nan and Grandad were shouting at him from the other side of the door, trying to get him to open up and telling him to calm down. I could hear them shouting from the back garden and came inside.

They couldn't get into the room because he was leaning against the door. Grandad wasn't a big bloke so he couldn't push the door open. Nan was freaking out and calling out to Dad to open the door. I started screaming for my dad to open the door. Then Dad started swearing and telling Nan to take me away because I didn't know what was going on. All I knew was my dad was upset over something.

Nan finally called the police and the ambulance. The ambulance bloke knew my dad from football. They'd played together in the Allerton team. He started talking to him to try to get him to open the door. They talked for a while and they kept it up. He managed to calm my dad down but then my dad went quiet and stopped talking back. That's when the ambulance man kicked the door in. Luckily they got him to hospital and pumped his stomach out to make him bring up everything he had swallowed. He came back to Nan's after that and lay low for a few days. He never talked to me about it and I never mentioned it again.

I sat down on a park bench and thought about my dad at that time in his life. I could see where he had come from, and that the pain was just too deep to handle. I guess he looked back at his life like I was looking at mine and just seeing a wreckage of people that was too hard to put back together.

I had no-one really to turn to except my friends. I needed someone out of my circle but I didn't have anyone. My dad and I were not really talking because I still hadn't forgiven him for selling Grandad's house.

I prepared a text message to send to all my friends and saved them. I knew from a line of contacts that someone could arrange a contract killing for me. I met up with a mate I knew who could get it organised and told him what I needed. This guy would do anything for me and I trusted him. I said to him there is something I need to talk to you about in private, can we meet?

We arranged to meet in the park.

'There's somebody that I need taking out.'

'Who is it Neil', he asked me.

'You don't know him,' I said. 'But can you sort it?'

'Of course,' he said. 'When do you want it to happen?'

'Next week,' I said. 'So how much will it be?'

'For you, it'll be a thousand dollars. I don't really care about the money Neil. I'll do it for you for free mate you know that.'

'Okay I will send you all the details,' I said.

'Sweet.'

And that was that.

I texted him all the details. He was to come Queen's Park near Randwick. He had to be there at a certain time. I described what the person's clothes would be that they were wearing—what I would be wearing. Once I sent the message I knew my days were numbered. Strangely, I actually felt relieved and started to enjoy my life. I spent as much time with Lillian as I could in that week. I felt numb and yet light-headed at the same time. I hoped that Lillian would understand why I had to do this, why I just couldn't see a better way out.

Three days before the due time for the hit I got a phone call from my mate asking me to meet up with him at Queen's Park. I agreed. When I got there I saw him sitting on the bench. I walked up to him to shake his hand but instead he stood up and he slapped me hard across the face. He started shouting at me: 'It's you, Neil, isn't it, it's you!'

'What is?' I shouted back

'It's you I'm doin' the hit on, isn't it, Neil? It's you!'

'No way,' I said and walked off.

He followed me, pushing me in the back, and shouting at me to tell him the truth.

'What, so you want me to shoot my own mate, do you? Are you alright or what Neil?' he kept shouting.

I started crying a little.

'What's up with you, Neil?' he said, talking quieter now. 'Why do you want me to do this?'

I broke down in front of him. I told him about my marriage breakdown and my anxiety about my daughter.

'Neil,' he said. 'Your missus is not worth it.'

We sat down on a bench. We talked all about it for hours until it got dark. I came around and got myself together. Finally I asked him how he had worked out it was me that he was supposed to hit up?

He told me that he knew I lived around Queens Park. And didn't I remember that when I had first moved here we would meet up there all the time? He said he worked it out when he realised I lived around the corner. He told me he would be keeping the text message that I sent to him to show people in case I tried to do something stupid like that again. I showed him the text messages I had got ready to send to my friends and we sat there and deleted them all.

After a while, we started laughing about it. He told me that when he slapped me across the face he was shitting himself that I would punch him back and he would be dead! I made a promise to myself never to let anyone make me feel that bad again.

My mate never told anybody about it. I owe a lot to him in more ways than one. If he hadn't caught me out, I would have ended my life there and then. And I would never have met Mariana.

13

Underbelly Celebrity

I could tell when someone had an argument with someone, or things were not working out in their life, by the way they behaved down at the club. Sometimes partners would come looking for them, and bust them right there and then, coming out of the toilets with the wrong person, or lots of the wrong people or even the wrong sex of person. Working in the clubs you see a lot of the highs and the lows of celebrity life, particularly the amount of coke, pills and alcohol some people consume.

When you are a celebrity, everyone wants a piece of you. I got a call from my mate Ahmad Elrich asking if I could help. It seemed that Tim Cahill, the Socceroo player, was in a bit of trouble. He was over in Australia on a break from Everton and when he went to Trademark someone in security had kicked him out and made a big fuss about it, while apparently manhandling him out the door.

'Well, what do you want me to do about it?'

'There's going be heaps in the media about it,' said Ahmad. 'Tim knows they won't put his side of the story, but he just wants to stop anything getting out about it.'

'Tell him to give me a call.'

Half an hour later, Timmy called. He said he was sorry to drag me into it, but he'd been at Trademark and one of the security guys was giving him and his mates a hard time all night. He didn't want make an issue out of it but he didn't want anything in the papers about it either. I called Poata, the licensee of Trademark, to see if he knew anything. Po said Timmy was in the VIP section all night drinking with a few friends and that his mates were just a bit noisy and they were asked to leave. Sounded harmless enough. Why were the papers involved and how did they get a tip-off? Po said you never know, somebody was probably trying to get some publicity about it or make a scene about the club. Maybe there were some journalists in the club who wanted an excuse to write a story.

'Po you know all that made-up stuff could damage Tim, you know?' I said. 'He could lose sponsorship contracts and get a fine from his club or anything. Anyway he's a great bloke and it will give him a bad name. We need to fix this up for him quick smart.'

Po called the papers and told them Timmy did nothing wrong the night he was in Trademark and didn't cause any trouble while he was at the club. That was the end of it. I got to know Timmy and we became good friends while he was over in the UK playing for Everton. He sent me a signed shirt, saying thanks for everything. Even though it was an Everton shirt I didn't hold it against him. I think he's a great player for Everton and for the Socceroos.

While I was working for John in 2010, the TV series *Underbelly* hit Channel 9 and rocketed through the ratings. John became a celebrity himself overnight. The 13-part TV series was all about Kings Cross and John as a young man, buying up clubs and doing business. It was a smash hit, and John became known as the 'King of Kings Cross'. It covered the time from 1988 and 1999, and the police corruption that lead to the massive Royal Commission in 1995.

Suddenly everyone wanted a picture with John or an interview with John, to put him in their show or on radio. The news program *A Current Affair* did a piece on him. His mate, radio DJ Kyle Sandilands, rang him and got him out of bed to do a live interview, YouTube pictures and movies of him took off, and he started to knock back offers to appear on TV shows. He put up a Facebook page and immediately got likes. Someone set up a twitter account for him and it has 39,000 followers.

The actor Firass Dirani was chosen to play John in *Underbelly: The Golden Mile*. Firass loved clubbing and he could certainly party hard. He would let his hair down after filming *Underbelly* until 3am. Maybe he was researching his role! Once I took him upstairs at Havana on Oxford Street.

'Hey, Neil.'

'What?' I said.

'I've heard a lot about you.'

'Yeah? All good I hope!'

'You're in the paper more times than I am.'

'Yeah, but you're in them for all the right reasons, I'm in them for all the wrong.' We'd catch up whenever we were free or he would come to the Cross and stand on the door and shout my name until security came and got me. In 2011, he won two Logie Awards, for the Most Outstanding New Talent and the Most Popular Male New Talent awards for his role in *Underbelly*. He did it really well. Firass is the nicest bloke.

John didn't seem to mind some of the attention, especially from the girls. Getting photos every two minutes with groups of females and the odd males. He had a fit body and a smile. So my job was doubled overnight— and as well as looking out for any nutcases that might to try to take him on, my job was to shield him from the media and people who wanted to talk to him and put him on air. Already celebrities were coming into his clubs, but suddenly he also got invited to celebrity parties all over Sydney. My life was busy! He's actually quite a shy person and, while he doesn't mind getting his picture taken, he gets nervous when the TV cameras appear.

Ben Fordham from another news program, called *Today Tonight*, came up to interview him in the main street of Kings Cross. John told me to stay close by when they came over and if the interview went on for too long, it was my job to let them know their time was up and get rid of them. He'd give me a signal when he'd had enough. So I put a bit of distance between us and I could see he was nervous about it. We were standing outside Porky's and the journalist began asking him questions.

He was laughing and joking with them and he looked comfortable. But I kept thinking when do I go over, do I leave it or not? He looked fine to me, so I left it. He wasn't going to give them a full-blown interview about his life though and he kept asking them to put their cameras down and just have a chat with him in the club. But they persisted and got a couple of quotes from him saying that Kings Cross was safe enough if 'you're a grown-up', and that the 'Police are fine. I think it was a bit overwhelming for them at the start, all the influx of people into Kings Cross, but they've got a hold of it now.'

Finally they left and he walked over to me.

'Why didn't you come over and get me!'

'Where was your signal?' I said. 'All I could see you doing was laughing and joking with them. You looked pretty comfortable to me.'

'You should've just come over and pushed them away!' he said.

'Well,' I laughed, 'I thought you wanted more camera time.'

He laughed. We took all the crew to Trademark for a few drinks. It wasn't enough that he had an interview that was basically about not having an interview! Then that story was reported on other TV programs about it being a non-event.

There was another guy who would walk around with us or be by John's side sometimes. Richie, Tongan Sam's nephew, was a top bloke and I mean that. We first met when I was working on the door at DCM's. He would work there with me but was brought in by John to be there just in case something went down. He would hang out at the club and just watch over us and hang around with us too.

Richie would be just quietly hanging around, unnoticed by anyone, even the cops. We hit it off straight away and became the best of mates. He is a family man who will put his family first before work. He was also Tongan Sam's nephew. What I like about Richie is that he doesn't try to be somebody he's not. He was a really nice guy but if you pissed him off Richie could fight and fight well. He was also a bloke who would go out of his way for you and help you in anyway he could. He was always there for me and if anyone had my back I know he did. He's another bloke who would do just about anything for John. John commanded that kind of loyalty from people without even asking. Richie started off being one of Sam's boys and then he would turn up with his uncle Tongan Sam with John.

One time when told me that he was being offered a chance to go on *MasterChef*. He said they came to him and offered him to be on the show. But he said there was no way he would go on the show as he can't cook. And it just wouldn't be right seeing John trying to make a pavlova with an apron on. So he said to me, do you want to go on it? I said, yeah I'll go on it, but I don't think he believed I could cook. I offered to cook for him to show him I could, but I don't think he wanted me to look like a dickhead if I went on there and I couldn't cook. So I never went on the show. In the end, one of his mates went on the show but he didn't make the cut.

When I started working at Trademark I was given the roll of overlooking the door and watching the staff. The same would go for the rest of John's venues. There was so much free shit given away by management and promoters that I didn't care about rattling someone's cage and having them run back to management about me. I thought it would show that I could be on to something and would watch them more. There were so many people on the take in all the venues, from security to bar staff to promoters—even the management sometimes, I reckon.

There was a promoter who I caught dealing and I told him to fuck off. Then one of the management staff asked me why he was barred. I told him, but within a week he was back in, so I knew straight away who was getting the shit off him if he was back without my knowing. A lot of people would take advantage that way when they started working at the venues. I even caught one promoter telling girls at the front of the venue that he was the manager, when really he was just a promoter on a Saturday night. The same promoter would run up a bar tab of $400, plus a night, giving free drinks to his mates. I soon put a stop to that.

There was one time when the Comancheros were showing their faces in the Cross a lot. John, Tongan Sam, the boys and I were all in Trademark at the time and John was in Piano Room, when I got a message from the doormen on the front door that about 30 Comancheros had just turned up across the road from Trademark and they are just looking over and that I'd better come and have a look. So I went to the front door to see and they were hanging on the corner looking over and more of them were turning up. I went back inside to find John and tell him what was going on. A few of the boys said maybe it would be best to get John out of the club and into his car in case something goes down, but John is not like that. He wanted to show his presence. So we all went outside to the front door of Trademark, but we all stayed close to John. We stood there for half an hour or so looking over but the Comancheros moved on after a while to a club they had just down the road. While this was going on, I messaged a few of the boys to give them a heads up. They came down straight away, about 20 of them, and we all went down to the club where the Comancheros were. When the Comancheros saw us outside they all came out and it was all on. We were all going punch for punch on each other until the cops came and we were split up. A few of the boys and I went to Hugo's to chill out for a bit.

I remember this one person who would go around the Cross and tell girls he was Fadi Ibrahim or John Ibrahim. The first time he did it was in DreamGirls. He came down and he had all the girls around him shouting them drinks and all of a sudden one of the girls came over to me and said, 'Hey, Neil, you know what John looks like, don't you?'

'Yeah, why do you ask?' She told me the guy handing out free drinks was telling everyone he was John. I started laughing. I walked over and said to him, 'How are you, mate? Can I have a word with you for a few moments, please.'

He said, 'Yeah, what's up?'

I said, 'Listen, John, or whatever your name is, you're out of here.'

He said to me, 'Do you know who I am?' I was thinking to myself, this is going to be so fuckin' funny when I tell him who I am. So I asked him who he was, as I wanted to make a show of this bloke in front of the strippers. He said, I'm John Ibrahim. I nearly choked from him actually saying that. So I told him who I was and did he know me? Straightaway he went, 'No, don't know you.' After that I dragged his little ass out of there ramming him into tables and chairs on the way out and throwing him into the stairs. Marcel and Jimmy quickly came down to see what was going on and grabbed him from me thinking I was going to maul this guy. I told him if I ever saw or heard of him using John's name again I will fuckin' flog the fuck out of you. The fucker did it again, but this time outside Trademark, telling the doorman he was Fadi. They messaged me to come out as they said Fadi is outside for you. I looked at my watch and thought, that's strange, he should be at home because of his home detention. When I got out there they pointed to the guy using Fadi's name. I grabbed him and said, 'What the fuck did I tell you?' and gave him the biggest fuckin' slap in the face outside Piano Room.

Being John's bodyguard had its perks, and without sounding big-headed, I don't think there is another doorman in Sydney that people know about as much as me. I never had to wait in any lines outside clubs and never paid for drinks. I was always given the best tables at restaurants and I was even given tickets to good quality functions, like the Melbourne Cup or the Aria Awards. When you ask someone about DCM's, yeah you have your DJs, but most people turn around and say they remember Big Neil from the door. I remember when I went the Aria Awards one year and I was walking down the red carpet with all these celebrities. All of a sudden, this group of people shout out, 'Neil, it's Neil from DCM's, go DCM's!' Plus I had Joel Madison behind me—it was fuckin' funny. He was probably going, who the fuck is he?

There was hardly a time that I couldn't get in anywhere. A lot of doormen knew me from years ago as it was. So they would look after me. Then there were the doormen who knew of me and were shit-scared to say no to me anyway. Then there were the managers of the venues who looked after me too. All these guys knew that if they ever came to one of the venues I looked after, I would treat them the same way back.

All the Cross clubs attracted a lot of celebrities and people from TV and the Kings Cross club and bar owners were treated like celebrities. I became friends with Peter Everett from the TV show *Ready Steady Cook* when I was working at DCM's. I would always joke and ask him when he was going to get me on his show. He set up a meeting for me with the producers, but a few weeks before we were due to go on they cancelled. I think they got cold feet about me being an underworld figure and *Underbelly* was on Channel 9, their rival.

Another person who I got really close with was Mark Bosnich, the Socceroos player. Mark is a workaholic—I don't think even his partner sees much of him as he travels around working for Fox Sports. He is the hardest person to get in touch with and takes weeks to reply to messages. I'd have more luck messaging the English Prime Minister than messaging Mark. Mark has the best sense of humour and his laugh is crazy. We've had some good times, me and him. When I had New Year's Eve parties at my old place in Neutral Bay, I would get him on the DJ set I had and we would do a bit of DJing and also karaoke. We'd both sing Vanilla Ice, with the dance moves to match. He is a legend. We have become really close, so close he is godfather to my son Cruz. The thing I like about Mark is that he is genuine.

I also got to know Kyle Sandilands. He started coming to Piano Room and then all of sudden he was kind of in-partnership. John would tell me to look after him while he was in the club and in the Cross. I would keep a close eye on him. John used to tell me that Kyle loved it when I looked after him. There was only one situation in Piano Room when someone put their arm around Kyle's neck a bit too much and made him feel uncomfortable and so I straight away grabbed him and removed him. Kyle is a top bloke.

Kyle's partner-in-crime Brian Mcfadden is also a funny bloke—nice bloke, knows how to party. Sometimes I couldn't keep up with him. We had some great times. And his ex, Delta Goodrem, was pretty great, too. She came to Piano Room a few times, but didn't really stay long. When she would leave I would always walk her to her car. One night her car was all the way down William Street, so you can imagine everyone looking at her and trying to get a picture with her.

I was also good friends with the singer-songwriter and TV presenter Ricki-Lee. We partied for a bit with her while I was living in Bondi. If she was out clubbing I would make sure she got looked after while she was in the Cross. I remember we went shot for shot at the Eastern one Wednesday night. We don't talk much anymore—top chick. Not sure why we don't talk anymore.

While *X-Factor* was on television, I would look after Guy Sabastian and Natalie Imbruglia. I already knew Guy, but I got to know him on more of a personal basis when looking after him. Natalie was a great person and we would talk for ages when she came to the Piano Room about living in the UK and her love for football. Everyone would say she liked the attention she was getting from me as I had to look after her while she was there. She liked me to walk her everywhere and make sure I stood by her. She's a really friendly person.

I met Salvatore Coco, who was acting in *Underbelly* as Sam Ibrahim. He was the host of the night at my wedding with Mariana. He did a great job. He came around to our place a couple times and I even cooked for him. Lucky person—I only cook for special people. In 2010, I met up with Sunny Alberton who wanted me to be in a TV series for him. We are good mates. Other people I have met or looked after while they are in the Cross are Richard Branson, Sonny Bill Williams, Potbelleez, Rapper Lil' Wayne and Ronan Keating. Ja Rule I especially enjoyed looking after. While he was at Trademark I remember him saying to me that he would love to have me back home looking after him. I was honoured he said that.

Just like in Liverpool bars and clubs, heaps of sports stars and footballers hang out at the bars and clubs in the Cross. A lot of footy players from the Tigers, Roosters, South Sydney, Dragons and Bulldogs come to the Cross. Benji Marshall was a regular at Piano Room on a Sunday night with a few other Tigers players. At first they all got on my nerves just coming in and getting pissed. Benji mellowed when he met his missus, and after that was pretty chilled when he came to Piano Room. I was good friends with Anthony Minichiello. My mate Lincoln played footy with him at the Roosters so I got to know him that way. I would always look out for him when he was out as he was a top bloke.

Meanwhile, my dad had moved to Spain to open up a wine bar/restaurant. He'd got married and seemd to be happy with his new partner. I felt glad for him, but I still felt hurt by things that had happened in the past. Then suddenly I got a call from his partner that he had been stabbed when he was walking home from his wine bar. I broke down. I felt so lonely and estranged from Dad, my real mate. I was lost for words and didn't know what to do. I asked her if I should come over but she said there is no need as he was stable and OK. It made me look at life a bit differently. That day I could have lost my dad and we weren't talking at the time. That would have killed me for the rest of my life if we had never made up and started talking again. If he had died, I wouldn't have been able to forgive myself. I was proud of my dad. Dad is still my hero. Luckily he was OK from the stabbing and recovered quickly.

Tiffani and I started proceedings for a divorce and it was messy, but settled pretty quickly. I'm still struggling with the terms of the settlement with my daughter. The court case for me to get access to my daughter Lillian, went on for over three years. It's drained me, and at the end of the day who's the winner? Someone isn't thinking that there is a little girl here who wants to see her mum and dad but her mum wants her all to herself, so Lillian misses out. In those three years I'd be lucky if I saw my daughter 10 times. It's been made hard for me and it shouldn't be like that. People become bitter because of splits, or bitter because of the new partner the ex-partner now has, or bitter because the child likes the new partner. Some people need to move on and get a life and stop taking it out on the child. Lillian loves me and misses me, and feels the same way about Mariana, but certain people need to deal with that and move forward. All the bullshit that came out in court from Tiffani saying I'm a bikie and a standover man for John Ibrahim and that if I have Lillian, she can't go near the following people cause they're bad, how do you work that out? Tiffani knew John before I did, she had sung in all his venues but John's a bad person? She doesn't have a clue what she's talking about. It should be about Lillian seeing her dad, not about his work. It shouldn't matter who I work for as long as I'm a good father to her. Hopefully 2013 brings me better luck and Lillian can come see me a lot more than she has. Hopefully things will sort themself out so I can be a dad to her again.

14

Not the Royal Wedding

Mariana Korac came to Piano Room a few times on a Saturday night. I noticed her because she really stood out in the crowd. She was tall and had beautiful big eyes. She had long dark hair and a stunning figure. She knew how to dress really well. When you looked at her it was wow! We didn't have a drink or anything, I would just look at her from afar and ask people who she was and if she was single. I must have told everyone that I wanted her. I noticed she was on a mate's Facebook page and I asked her to be a friend as well. She accepted. One morning when I had just got home from working, it was about 7am on a Sunday morning, and she was the only person online. I asked her why she was up so early? She messaged me back 'I am doing spring-cleaning!' We chit-chatted for about half an hour and then I asked her out for dinner.

'I don't go out with bad boys and I hear a lot about who you are.'

I just said, well don't get too excited. At the end of the day I am just Neil. It's just a job I do.'

She was in real estate and had done some acting as well. She'd won heaps of model contests for Miss Croatia and Miss Bondi and just looked stunning in pictures. On the night we were going to have our first date, she was guest judge at a modelling function down at Wooloomooloo. I actually had the best time there, even though she was busy judging. We went to Trademark after for a drink and met up with a few of our friends. While I was on the dance floor with my mates she played a trick on me by pretending to leave. I panicked and ran after her thinking she was leaving, but she was hiding to see what I would do. I felt like a right prat, but good in a way. The next night, I asked to have the Saturday off. I hadn't taken a Saturday off for god knows how long. I was always working on a Saturday night—it was the main night of the week. It was extremely rare for me but I was really excited about this girl and I wanted to give it a really good try. I had spent the whole day at her place and didn't want to leave her and she didn't want me to. So I took her to Luna Park. What a night we had—everything went right. I even won her a massive teddy bear.

I booked the restaurant for the next evening and let her know. She messaged me saying she had a car crash. I thought she was trying to get out of it. So I messaged her.

'Are you trying to avoid me?' I asked.

She laughed. 'It's not that bad! I just can't drive! Can you come over to my place instead?'

I went over and took her out to Luna Park and won her loads of teddy bears. I virtually moved in with her straight away. It just felt right and we connected so well. We hated being apart and I must admit it was hard going to work sometimes, as I enjoyed being with her and I hated leaving her.

Sundays was my night off. Sometimes Mariana and I would go to Piano Room or sometimes we would go somewhere else. One Sunday we heard that the Comancheros had just done a national run and were coming into the Cross after it. So I went into work just in case something went down. While I was sitting at the bar, the Middle Eastern crime squad came in and saw me sitting there. 'Why is Neil here tonight?' they asked the manager. He just told them I was having a few drinks.

They walked through the whole club and then asked me to come outside with them. When I got outside they started searching me.

'Why are you here, Neil?' they kept saying.

'I am having a few drinks, that's all,' I kept replying.

'Wallet and mobile please. Undo your trousers and take your shirt off.'

When they found my car keys, they asked me where it was parked.

'Down there, in Victoria Street.'

'If you don't tell me where it is I will find it myself,' said the copper.

'I'll take you there, I've got nothing to hide,' I said. It was typical of them, searching me for stuff they knew I didn't have.

When we got to the car they went through everything, and I mean everything, from boot to engine and seats. All they found was a bikini belonging to Mariana, so they made jokes about her. I held it in and told them she wasn't their type. They had no right talking about her like that. It was all such a waste of time. In the end nothing happened, but if I spoke about their missus like they spoke about Mariana they would have found a way of arresting me for sure.

It was usually the Gang Squad taskforce, called Raptor Squad, who gave me a hard time. They would always stop me and ask what I was doing in the Cross, or wherever I was, even turning up at my unit and even once coming to Mariana's work looking for me. They make out that they're your friend and have a laugh and a joke with you to butter you up, but really they are waiting to pounce and get information or get you for anything they can. Once they told me I had to leave the Cross as they feared I was there to be a standover man and maybe inflict harm on certain rivals.

When my mates and I would go out, we'd go through five to eight bags of coke a night and if we ran out I would organise more to be dropped off wherever we were, but I would never do it in front of Mariana. I didn't even tell her I took drugs until later on in our relationship. We had a New Year's Eve party at our apartment—all the boys came and we kept going into the front of the unit or bathroom, so she kind of caught on.

On Mariana's birthday, I filled our unit with balloons waiting for Mariana to come home for her to surprise her. I got a couple of guys to help me on the road leading to the Harbour Bridge to put up a massive banner to say 'I love you Mariana, from your Neil'. We did that the night before at 2am in the morning. When she got home I played our song—KC & JoJo's 'All my life'— it was perfect. Plus a few nice presents were scattered around the unit for her to find. I think I did well that night, but she is worth it. When I decided to ask Mariana to marry me I organised to hire the bird show at Taronga Zoo. I organised with the bird keeper to get the engagement ring attached to a hawk and they would ask someone in the crowd to stand up, while the hawk flew to her with the ring and then I would stand up in front of everyone and ask her to marry me. I was panicking that the bird would drop or lose the bloody ring, which was two and a half carat dimond ring. It was the ring she wanted from day one of looking, so I knew she would be happy when she got it. I managed to get all her family to the zoo without Mariana thinking anything of it and a few of my mates came too. There were even people in the crowd watching the bird show who were regulars at Trademark. When she said yes I was the happiest man alive and they released 30 white doves.

At that time I was also thinking about getting myself into shape to do some pro-boxing fights. But then I realised that the fights were too close to when I was getting married and if I got a cut or bruised face that would be no good for the wedding photos. I was so disappointed about not being able to box. I had trained so hard for it. But we had decided on a big wedding, and for some extra cash we agreed to let *OK!* magazine have an exclusive on it. It was going to be a big event so I wanted everything to be perfect.

We sat down together and wrote down the guestlist for the day. I looked at the people on Mariana's side of the list and then I looked at mine. Mariana was inviting all of her large Croatian family, friends of friends and lots of people from her childhood and school days. On my side, there were heaps of doormen, John and Fadi Ibrahim, some bikies, some celebrites and some known Kings Cross identities. Every day leading up to the wedding I kept thinking about what her family would say when they leant across to look over to my side of the wedding. They'd wonder, who the hell is Mariana marrying!

It came time to choose my wedding party—the best man and groomsmen. It was a hard decision, as I didn't have any of my family in Australia. I wanted to make sure that I picked the right guys, people who meant something to me.

The Muscle

My groom's party was Ahmad Elrich, Fadi Ibrahim, Dave Freeman, Eddy Asotasi and Gregor Agic. The bridesmaids were Manuela, Rennee, Lisa, Carla and Tessa.

My mates from the Cross had become my second family. First, I wanted to ask Fadi to be a groomsman. I wanted him to be part of my day. The problem was he was on home detention. He couldn't come to the buck's night even though he tried to get a pass from the courts. They turned him down for that, but he kept trying to get a pass for the wedding itself and in the end, at the very last minute, they allowed him to come. I asked Eddy to be a groomsman and he accepted.

Ahmad Elrich had become a really great mate and we were never apart. We would hang out together whenever we could, he was like a brother to me (but I was the good-looking brother!) That's how I treated him. I asked Ahmad to be a groomsman, and I also had him down as a possible best man. Gregor was also asked to be a groomsman. I invited Dave Freeman to the wedding as well. I was so glad that he could come, as he always calmed me down and relaxed me if anything got tense. It doesn't surprise me that he is doing great business with the revamped Lady Lux, which he turned into the Backroom Bar.

I asked John Ibrahim to be my best man. It was a way of saying thank you, to show him that it had been such an honour to work for him. In the lead up to the wedding, a few people told me John was getting nervous about having to be the best man and delivering the speech. 'He'll get over it,' I kept saying to them. Mariana had a chat with John and told him how much it would mean to me for him to be best man. He kept pulling me aside and trying to get out of it. But I was determined. I kept thinking, 'Oh well, it's just one day, John, you will get over it and surely you won't let me down.' He even said to me that he would pay for my whole wedding if he just didn't have to be best man. I should have taken him up on his offer!

I decided I was going to sing a song for Mariana at the wedding, and for a solid three months I kept going over Robbie Williams' 'Better Man' while I was alone in our unit. I kept singing in the car or in the lounge room while no-one was around. In fact I was more nervous about singing in front of my friends than to Mariana. They'd see a side of me that they never did see. They'd see a lovey-dovey Neil, but it was Mariana's day and that's why I didn't care what they thought.

Not long before the wedding I got a phone call at 2am in the morning from someone saying they were from the Comancheros asking me questions about myself and John and even Tongan Sam. They wanted John's number and Sam's, but I told them I didn't have them. I kept hanging up on them and they would call back. Then they asked if I was John Ibrahim's bodyguard. I said what kind of a question is that, you're not very switched on if you don't know. They said they wanted me to tell them. I replied by saying mate, you have my number and you know my name but you don't know what I do. I said why don't you Google me that will tell you and I hung up. He called back saying you want to be smart, Neil, then if we see you walking next to John at the weekend we shoot you and come and get your model missus. My buck's weekend was coming up and I told my mates what had happened. I wanted to cancel it so I could be with John after that phone call as I was thinking they were going to do something to him if I wasn't there. Nothing happened. Who knows what they were on about.

On the day of the wedding everything was in place. I was getting dressed when I got a message from Nassar to say that John was going to put Dave Freeman in his place as best man. Nassar said John just wants to relax and enjoy your wedding and not have to make a speech. I was so disappointed that he had let me down when this had meant so much to me. To do it on the day of my wedding killed me. The one thing I had asked from him since I had been working with him and he had let me down. But I also understood that he hated being in the public eye and hated giving speeches. In lots of ways I shouldn't have been surprised. I remember at Frank Amante's daughter's christening a few months before the wedding he was so nervous about being godfather and making a speech at the reception. He hates that kind of thing. I should hit him up for the wedding cost for doing that! I called Mariana to let her know what had happened. I didn't want her turning up at the church and not seeing John as best man. I quickly went and got Ahmed and asked him to do it instead. At the end of the day he deserved to be my best man, even though I wished that I had written his speech for him (sorry mate!).

The Muscle

Everyone was waiting at St Michael's church, North Sydney for the groom's party to arrive but Mariana turned up first. Isn't it supposed to be the bride who is late to the wedding, not the groom? I was an hour late! Poor Mariana thought something had happened to me. I was stressing her out on her big day.

Before Ahmad, Eddy and Gregor and I left the hotel to pick up Fadi in the limousine, we had to wait for Dave Freeman to turn up. Then when we picked up Fadi we had to go and sign in at the police station in Chatswood as he was under house arrest. We pulled up outside and went into the station all dressed up to sign him out. I wished we had taken a photograph of that. It would have been the funniest picture ever.

We all squashed into the limo, and then on the way to the church the driver took the wrong exit, taking us on to the Harbour Bridge heading south instead of north. My mobile phone was going off, with the priest's number flashing continuously, but I didn't want to answer it so I let it ring out. I was worried what Mariana would be thinking. I was told she did five laps around the block while she was waiting for me. It was a really hot day in Sydney that day and with the dress she was wearing in that heat she would have been cursing me under her breath.

There were two helicopters following our wedding cars, packed with media. They were there hovering over the church and there were journalists all over the place. I even had four big security guards looking after Mariana. They were to not let any media near her or take photos of her. They did the same at the reception too. When we finally got to the church, we got out of the limo and sorted ourselves out. John came to see us at the back of the church. 'Neil, I thought you weren't going to show up for a minute there!'

When Mariana came down the aisle all I did was cry. She walked down to Robbie Williams' song 'Angels', I couldn't hold it in and all the boys were looking at me while I was crying my eyes out. I didn't care, she looked so beautiful. I couldn't wait to marry her and for her to become Mariana Cummins.

It was a beautiful wedding. Everyone I wanted was there to celebrate it with me, although nobody came from Liverpool.

I got up in front of everyone and sang my song. I think I did an all right job. It came from the heart and shows how much she means to me and how much I love her. It was something I had thought about doing ever since we set the date for the wedding. I'm no Robbie Williams (well, maybe on the dance floor) but on that night I tried my best to be.

Towards the end of the night we were told the cops had got wind of the wedding venue and had turned up outside. There was two cop cars and two undercover cop cars sitting off outside. Nearly everyone who left the reception got pulled over. Fuckin' coppers—you can't do anything without them turning up uninvited to try to ruin things.

The wedding made the afternoon news. They called it the 'other Royal Wedding', because there were so many underworld figures there.

A few weeks later we were back at work and John called me out the back of Piano Room to the loading dock. 'I want to talk to you, Neil,' he said. 'I like working with you, don't get me wrong. I want to ask you a question. Is this what you really want to do?'

'What do you mean John?'

'I mean you have a beautiful wife, and you might want to start a family. Do you want this shit in your life? Why don't you take a month off and take a holiday? Talk to me when you get back.' He'd been told the cops had it in for me and wanted me out of the Cross and were looking for ways to get rid of me.

I was shocked. What was he doing? Was he giving me the sack? I had been so loyal to him. I had turned down heaps of work offers to work with him. I was shocked.

When I got home I told Mariana what John had said. 'Don't you understand?' she said. 'He's giving you a get-out clause.'

15

Cross Detox

I felt lost and rejected. I had looked after John for 10 years and I had given him everything! I was confused. Was he giving me the sack? No, he wasn't. Mariana said to me again: 'He's giving you an option to get out Neil. He's giving you the easy way to leave.' I hung around the house like a caged lion, and sent him messages, asking him if he wanted me around. I didn't turn up for work, I went to the gym instead.

'Relax, Neil' he texted back. 'Take a holiday and relax.'

So I did. I decided to take a break for three months and take it from there. Take a holiday. I could always go back. What have I got to lose? Sound familiar?

When Mariana became pregnant, I wanted a chance to be a 'normal' family man, and I really wanted to be there for them. But I was really close to all the boys and the scene was my life. I had been doing it for 14 years, Monday to Sunday with 14-hour shifts! But I had to let it go. I needed to focus on my family and find other things to do. I just wanted to rest.

I missed the contact with the boys and everyone in the circle, but I had to go cold turkey. Otherwise I would just be back there in two weeks. I had to stop all contact with everyone, including John and Fadi. Don't get me wrong, it was hard. Sometimes I wanted to send text messages to them all and see what they were up to. Sometimes I just wanted to get in the car and go for a drive up to the Cross. But I didn't. I knew if I said hello to one person I would have to contact them all and it would end in a bitchfight, with people saying 'How come you messaged this guy and not me', and so on.

For the first six months I just stayed at home and did nothing. It was really hard to sleep. I couldn't get into a routine as I had been working on weekends and nights for so long. I was used to starting work at 9pm and then going to skeep at around 7am when I got home, sleep for about four to five hours and then hang out with the boys during the day, ready to start work again.

I just stayed up, watching TV until the early hours of the morning. I was really bored. I started going to the gym for three hours instead of two, and really didn't know what to do with myself at night. Then I decided to stop going to the gym as well. My body needed a rest too. I have pushed it so much over the years to keep in shape to maintain my physical shape, stay on the door and go out walking with John.

When Mariana went into labour we nearly lost our son. Mariana's blood pressure went down and the umbilical cord had got tangled around our baby while he was still inside. His heartbeat was faint and they were going to stick a needle into his head to try to calm him down, but Mariana and I didn't want that. So they did an emergency caesarean and at last he was born. Both Mariana and my son Cruz were fine and healthy. We spent New Year's Eve on the balcony of the hospital watching the fireworks, just the three of us. Straightaway I went and got his name tattooed across the back of my shoulders. I didn't want to be anywhere else but with Cruz. Everything else could wait. Here was my son and I wanted to be here with him. I loved waking up to him in the middle of the night and feeding him so Mariana could sleep. He was a little mini me. He was everything to me. I now felt relaxed and happy within myself that I had a great wife and family.

I knew a lot of people in the Cross but I was still surprised when I found out who my real mates were and who had just been using me for my contacts, after I had left the Cross. Some people did get in touch with me to see if I was okay. But lots of people just didn't care.

The Muscle

I don't really take drugs anymore as I don't party like I used to. Plus being in the scene and in the industry you get embroiled in it. Yes, I take steroids, but as for pills and coke, no. After my breakdown, sI felt better. I nearly made the wrong choice by taking my life. The right choice was leaving my marriage to tiffani. I was psycially drained from it and I was never myself. The Neil everyone knew.

I know that I worked my way up the ladder slowly and surely in my career. I did it the right way, not by using people or dropping names. I worked my ass off to get to where I was. I have met a lot of jealous people out there who didn't like that. But all my experiences have made me a stronger person and I know how to pick my friends now. Your friends are people who stand by you and don't ask for anything in return. Right now my best friend is my wife Mariana.

A few things happened that had made it a little easier to leave my job with John. A few people had been hanging out in the circle that I didn't get on with. I didn't want to work with them—I felt they didn't have my back. There was some jealousy and some people were trying to push me out. They didn't want me too close. It didn't feel right anymore, which was a shame as I loved my job and loved working for John.

After a while, I was offered a job as door host at Fusion Nightclub in Cronulla. I thought it would be fun to get back into it again and the club was relaxed. The people who worked there were great and a few of the doormen knew me. One actually used to come to DCM's and he told me he became a security guard because of me. I had a lot of fun working at Fusion, even though some people thought John owned it! I stayed at Fusion for about six months and I was grateful for the time they gave me there. But I started to want to get into a bigger club and it was giving my itchy feet.

I started doing a little bit of debt collecting around Sydney and Queensland. While I enjoyed doing it, it was taking me down a path I didn't really want to be going down. Sometimes I would be called on to collect money from high-profile people or businesses. I remember one time, I made an appointment under a false name to see a broker in an office in Sydney, who owed someone $123,000. When I got to the office, he finally came out to see me and took me into the boardroom. He sat down and said, 'How can I help you? What kind of business are your starting?'

When I told him he owed me $123,000 he laughed and said he owed no-one anything. He was the kind of businessman who thinks that he knows everything. So I told him again, 'You owe me $123,000'. When he lied to my face again, I pulled out the paperwork that had his signature, business name and the amount he owed on it. I also told him that I knew of his sister, who had a very high profile, and if this wasn't sorted out soon, I would take her name and his to the media. Within three days I received a phone call from him and an arrangement was made to collect on the debt. Still to this day, I get phone calls or messages to see if I can do a collection job for someone or put the heavy on someone.

While I was collecting, I was separating myself from my Cross personality and who I had been as John Ibrahim's bodyguard. And I found out who my true friends were.

I started hanging out with someone I thought was a friend, as I had know him for so long, but I had mostly been friends with his brother. He and I did a bit of debt collecting together and I had a few business deals I put to him. I thought he was someone I could trust him. But I guess you can't trust anyone these days, not even people you thought w your friends or had worked alongside for years. I gave this bloke—let's call him Mr B—$24,000 for a business deal and moved the money into his account. But what do you know, it went missing.

No matter how much I tried to sort it out and find were the money had gone, the damage was done. He had ripped me off. Doing that to me was like shooting me in the back. He hadn't just affected me, but my wife as well, as this was going to be a family business.

A good friend of mine was ripped off by Mr B a few days before it had happened to me, but I didn't know about it.But because of what Mr B did, my good friend stopped talking to me. I had put in a good word for Mr B and my friend had been ripped off, ruining a very close friendship.

I was very close to Mr B's brother and if I had gone straight to his brother and told him what he had done, he would have been killed. But his brother is locked up and I don't need to put more stress on him. All I can say is every dog has his day and one day, hopefully, fuckin' karma will get Mr B. The fuckin' prick ruined a friendship with someone who was truly like a brother to me and one of the best friends I have had. Hopefully one day we can be friends again.

After this, I decided to get out and get back to what matters to me most—my family. I want to spend more time with my wife, my son and also my daughter. After leaving the Cross I was asked to do some filming for *A Current Affair* on doormen and nightclubs down in Wollongong, walking the streets and talking about situations that happen on the doors. I really enjoyed doing it. While filming, all the doormen and the cops, who had been used to seeing me down at the Cross with all the boys, must have been wondering what the fuck I was up to with a film crew.

Maybe I am like my dad. He has been kicked back a bit. He still has Jalons restaurant in Liverpool and from what I hear he is enoying it. I think he just wants to do something mellow. He is enjoying his bar and restaurant in Spain as well. He goes between both of them each week to see how they are running.

If I had one wish in life it would be to have Nan and Grandad alive again. I know this might sound weird to some people but I miss them more than anything else in the world.

Above all, I can say I enjoyed my time in the Cross and working for John. I wouldn't change a thing. The biggest thing that I found after working in the industry for nearly 14 years is that there is no loyalty. Doing what I did, I lost friends and even family because I put work and other things first. That was because I loved my work and loved doing what I did, which was looking after John and his family. I worked my ass off to get to where I got. Now I look at who is looking after him and wonder would they take a bullet, would they stand up to anyone that crosses his path and would they be loyal. I was all three and I can say that proudly. It was never a money thing with me. No disrespect to the boys who are walking with him, but I look at some pictures that I have seen and it's like they all want is to wear their expensive clothes and just hang out with John and be seen with him. Not look out for him and watch his back. I call them the Armani Boys for the way they are with him. All except Tongan Sam.

The Cross is not what it seems. When you next go out to Kings Cross step back and have a look in the background not at the person next to you. Everyone seems to miss what the Cross is really like. Now I'm out of it I can see it for what it is. It entices you and sucks you in. I've met some great people there and some bad-ass people. It's been one massive roller coaster ride that's for sure.

But I never say never. Maybe one day I will be walking the Cross again. Maybe I will be looking after John, maybe not. Who knows what my next move is? Maybe I will open my own club on the Cross one day. For now I have a few things up my sleeve to do. But if it happens, you'll be the first to know.

Acknowledgements

To my beautiful wife, Mariana, and my son, Cruz. You both bring so much happiness to my life. Mariana, you are always there for me, through thick and thin. You stand by me all the time and I love you for everything you have done for me since I have met you. You are special and I don't know what I would do without you. I love you. To Cruz, my little boy. I love being with you every day and watching you grow. If anyone has calmed me down it has been you coming into my life. I love you so much.

To my dad, without your love and guidance there wouldn't be a story here for the telling. You were always there for me as a kid and only wanted the best for me. You have always been proud of me no matter what I have done and I thank you for that.

To my late nan and grandad even though you are not here anymore, I know you are looking down on me and watching over me as if you were here. You are never out of my mind or thoughts and I hope I have done you proud.

To my daughter, Lillian, thank you for coming into my life and bringing my so much joy when I see you. Hopefully soon I can see you more often and we can be close again.

To my school friends and my mates from boyhood, thanks for the exciting times when growing up.

To my best mate, Lee Burns, we have known each other since we were six years old and even though we live 15,000 miles away from each other our friendship is still as strong as when we were kids.

Acknowledgements

To my soccer mates, who have always been there for me, even after I finished playing—Steve, George, Azza, Jason, Hughsie and Billy.

To everyone at New Holland Publishers with special thanks to Fiona for her patience and support.

To all the venues, managers and licensees I have worked with. Thanks for having the trust in me to run your doors.

To all the doorman I have worked with, looked after or have got to know. Thanks for having my back, in particular Wayne, Fraser, Pat, Marcel, Jimmy, Fono and the boys from the door of Trademark—Levi, Mo, Scotty, Tangi, Ziad and Timmy.

To all the patrons that I got to know and have knocked back over the years. Thanks for the memories.

To all the DJs I have had the pleasure of meeting and becoming friends with: Micky D, Charlie Brown, Ace, Toby Neal, John Devecchi, Cadell and Potbelleez.

To all my close friends: Adam Osman, Craig, Cookie, Lincoln, Mick, Richie, Ahmed Elrich, Mark Bosnich. I thank you for being there as my friends.

To all the boys: Aka, Alan, Alla, Crazy Dave, Farzi, Fred, Wajdi, Tongan Sam and Big Fadi. Thanks for being there when needed.

To the media people for the good and bad things you have written about me. Particular thanks to Jonathan, Tito, Kai, Jonica and Monique.

Thanks to Dave Freeman for always being there for me and for being a great friend.

Also a special thanks to my friend and father figure old Frank. You have a heart of gold and you would always go out of your way for me. You looked after me and guided me and I'm grateful for everything.

And, finally, thanks to The Family—the Ibrahim family—Sam, Michael, Fadi and John. Thanks for giving me the chance to show you what I could do and the chance to work and look after you all when needed. Thank you for believing in me and trusting me to look after your wellbeing, it was a privilege to work for you. I have the utmost respect for every one of you.

First published in 2013 by
New Holland Publishers
London • Sydney • Cape Town • Auckland

www.newhollandpublishers.com

The Chandlery Unit 114 50 Westminster Bridge Road London SE1 7QY
1/66 Gibbes Street Chatswood NSW 2067 Australia
Wembley Square First Floor Solan Road Gardens Cape Town 8001 South Africa
218 Lake Road Northcote Auckland New Zealand

A catalogue record of this book is available at the British Library and at the National Library of
Australia

ISBN: 9781742573946

10 9 8 7 6 5 4 3 2 1

Publisher: Fiona Schultz
Writer: Lliane Clarke
Project editor: Jodi De Vantier
Designer: Tracy Loughlin
Cover design: Kimberley Pearce
Proofreader: Meryl Potter
Production director: Olga Dementiev
Printer: Ligare Book Printers Sydney

Follow New Holland Publishers on
Facebook: www.facebook.com/NewHollandPublishers